Build, Engage & Connect

ADVANCED TWITTER GUIDE

To my online community on Twitter,

this book is dedicated to you.

About The Author

Starting his career 20 years ago as an artist who loved computers and technology - since his father has been an IT professional since the late 60s - Sharif Sourour, when converging his skills of art and talents of technology together, landed his first professional role of graphic designer naturally in his teens.

Later in his young adulthood, he turned to his other passion, music, and was inspired to write song after song during his stint in Tokyo working in sports media. After writing hundreds of tunes and accompanying lyrics, he registered 140 of them back in his home country with the Songwriters Association of Canada and eventually got far enough to have one of his songs, *True Love*, published with Ambition/Fortitude/Decca a subsidiary of Universal Music Group (UMG) performed by singer Paulini Curuenavuli with her claim to fame being her runner-up status in the first Australian Idol and her highly successful role as part of the Young Divas. She recently starred in *The Masked Singer* Australia and in the musical version of *The Bodyguard*, playing Whitney Houston's iconic role.

Marrying his Japanese girlfriend, Sharif really started to hustle to try and figure out how he could have a career or business to support his new coming family. He ended up moving to British Columbia forfeiting a burgeoning modelling career that had been growing for him in Tokyo, published in men's casual and stylish fashion magazines before he had met his future wife to see if he could take his TV, Media and Technology skills to Vancouver, Hollywood North to potentially secure a stable job there.

It was a scrappy and rough start but with a constant drive to build the momentum he took it off the ground eventually offering 200-300+ pieces of valuable content for free at an average of 1 hour per live stream session available on periscope plus; interviews, music, top articles across the web, embedded videos on Twitter earning 10s of thousands of views put together aside from a wealth of video on YouTube. He went deep on social media for these skills after a stint back in college for several terms of Computer Engineering in Ottawa.

From there he discovered the number one high-value art one could develop in marketing and business, the content strategy that multiplied his engagement percentage by 10 times! Now he not only knew how to grow a following but how to engage that following and build a culture; a valuable ability sought out by the top marketers and leaders of the world. His platform has allowed him to connect to people like you, experts and top influencers in their niche globally.

5

Personal Twitter Story

The year was 2011, I was living on my own as a bachelor in Tokyo and after struggling with becoming a professional artist while learning a foreign language, doing part-time, technical and creative work; I was learning about the various new popular platforms online like Youtube which is where I first learned to work in TV a couple of years prior in New York City. Among those platforms was Twitter where I began exploring to discover the fascinating Twitter-verse.

At first I played around with different kinds of Tweets, direct messaging other users, tagging them in tweets, posting shortened links to external images. Twitter was not capable of displaying images locally so we would have to include a link. In the really early days links could not even be clicked on! You would have to copy and paste the website addresses to get to the pages. How times have changed! Nowadays new Twitter users are graced with a load of features including posting direct images, animated GIFs, videos, and polls. Now we can even stream on Twitter using Periscope!

Twitter, once the pioneer in minimalist micro-blogging, exclusive to text messages out into the cyber galaxy at a limit of 140 characters, is now a full fledged personal media channel interface, keeping up with and in some ways surpassing the feature-rich social media platform, Facebook. Though Twitter may not boast over a billion user profiles, it has now become a top news source in social media above Reddit while Facebook's huge user base has become more stagnant with the popularity of Instagram. On top of this, it is probably much easier to reach many more people with more content more often on Twitter than in Facebook from your own profile, you are not forced into using paid ads like Facebook demands - to match the effectiveness of e-guerrilla tactics - while your skills at using the platform will increase the value of your account, being able to reach much more people purely through organic means than not only Facebook but now Instagram since its organic engagement has recently declined for posts. Twitter just flaps by quickly to reach your contacts with less barriers or distractions while still giving you all you need to share content in multiple ways albeit quirkier.

After finding it was difficult to be found and engaged with in my early days on the platform along with my inability to quickly learn its simplistic interface, those first stages were a slow struggle to comprehend how to reach more people on the platform, but even as far back as 2011 there were highly experienced Twitter users who were not already well-known celebrities or public figures, who had instead already mastered, through their own trial and error, the secrets to dominating on the platform in their own way, so this gave me hope that the answers were out there. With a few hundred followers, mostly pulled from other sources like my email and Facebook, I enjoyed using the platform, sharing pictures, thoughts and findings during my time living in the land of the rising sun while watching the platform grow into its more mature and fully functional state. Somewhere along my journey, the next year I was finally dating again and found myself in a steady relationship, from there I knew it was time to get serious.

While networking and learning the industry in Vancouver, BC with my wife, at the time only our first child had been born, I began to leverage social media to increase my connections in the video production, VFX and animation industries in Canada's *Hollywood North* expanding from my experiences working at the TV station in New York (NTD) and at a magazine in Japan (World-TT). Furthermore I began becoming motivated to start my own business. With the help of my experiences shadowing a successful entrepreneur (Kean Wong) in Manhattan who also worked with the TV station and the resources he provided me, I began developing ideas and strategies while researching the kind of media and entertainment business desirable to create at the time.

Ending up working for a small independent music label in Burnaby, part of the lower mainland of Vancouver, I was working on their websites in WordPress. With web development experience before, it was my first time using the platform, so my experience proved to be highly valuable giving me a lot of hands-on practice gaining familiarity with the platform. At the same time I was trying to run my own website on a completely different platform customized by a 3rd-party developer. Unfortunately the platform was not only completely different than WordPress, but also unlike any platform I had used before… attempting to adjust and maintain my own website simultaneously became an organizational mess! Throughout this stressful time I managed to find a way to build a large list of email contacts which is growing to this day by buying a course through a social media advert. That course, though focused on LinkedIn, also featured a book on Twitter.

After going through the entire program and applying everything I had learned, happily applying my new Twitter knowledge within a matter months my account went from growing a couple of hundred followers to nearly a couple thousand. My friends amazed, I felt pretty satisfied with myself. A few years later in Ottawa I was upping my skills by studying in college, only applying the principles learnt about Twitter on and off.

After a few years since gradually applying those principles to Twitter, my followers now were over 20,000 and I had already gone through several semesters of college. It all of a sudden hit me and I got an "Aha!" moment, I thought "Why don't I apply these principles every single day, and take it further?" and I did just that, from there my account started to grow at a rapid rate. However it was not all of a sudden a free ride, though my follower count was going fast, my methods for achieving it were very tedious and labour-intensive. I also did not get much engagement for my posts and had trouble really connecting with my audience. I knew there had to be more to it. Truly going above and beyond, not only applying everything I knew, but exploring further, experimenting and getting into the nitty gritty of the data became paramount. What makes people tick? Most importantly… how do you cultivate meaningful relationships for deep connections between one another? Answering those questions was really going to bring intrinsic value to mastering Twitter.

Traffic

My engagement began to grow adding meaning to having a following in the first place! I started to step out of my comfort zone, started to take advantage of the fact I followed back most of my followers, constantly watching what they were posting live throughout the days, reaching out, liking, tweeting, replying, discussing, debating, switching to direct messages, and even connecting outside of Twitter, only starting to realize how amazing of a platform it really is. Going deeper, expanding my sources for tracking data and all along Twitter itself developed their own analytics tool Twitter Analytics. It is not that I would not pay for tools, it is just nice to have a just-as-viable free option to get my feet wet as to the actual work involved. Beyond this I started to learn about how to do advanced searches on Twitter, beyond just hashtags and lists. Why I would get engagement and traffic from people who do not follow me or how I would attract new followers without finding them. I started to realize Twitter is a whole world onto itself which could possibly be taught as a college course or university program.

That is what is relevant today. Being able to master today's information age online through the windows to a majority's eyes, the computer screens, smart phones, tablets and other smart devices; your doorway to the hearts and souls from people living on the other side of the world - maybe even to someone living right next door! This way everyone is your neighbour while everyone likewise has the authority to remain private if they so choose just as well regardless of how close or far they may be from each other at any given moment. It has never been as accessible to connect through the internet as today. This is truly the age of opportunity and my; discussions, polls, metric tracking, research, feedback and sought advice have all led me to the same conclusion… people want to know how it is one can consistently grow a Twitter profile like a rock star, as if there is some special sauce, magic spice or secret hack to achieve it. As usual however, there are no magic pills, but just common sense practices you can put into place today to achieve real results.

It is just like exercise, if you learn from an experienced trainer who has been through all the trial and error and is deep into the nuances of his practice, with a complete, continuously growing and empowering perspective on his system, applying that person's teaching will give incredibly fast results. I have even seen such an example online for myself, having read the story of an average man following the exact same regimen as Dwayne Johnson and in a short time, he also started to achieve big fitness results quickly. The important point is that he actually followed the same routine and that thankfully when it comes to Twitter you do not have to put yourself nearly through the pain of the kind of regimen it takes to train like *The Rock*. Instead you only need a maximum of an hour a day to really grow your following and create the basis for your own full-fledged media channel online. One that has the power to drive traffic to your blog, website or any place you want!

Intro

"Everyone thinks they missed the boat, but over the years I've always found a new boat."
- Ezra Firestone

Congratulations! You are on the start of a whole new journey to completely change your life with the incredible power of Twitter networking, marketing and business. The book you are now reading contains all the secrets developed over nearly a decade of research, trial and error, practice and development in the aspects of growing a following, engaging that audience with a proper content strategy and finally building relationships with those interested with what you have to offer in order to convert your prospects into customers that not only buy once, but always come back for more.

How can you do this? With the power of this book you will go from someone who may or may not know something about the platform to one that has built his or her own community around one's niche and interests. Twitter still maintains an active, living, breathing, user base of approximately 300+ million people strong (*Source: https://blog.hootsuite.com/twitter-statistics/*), which at one time was considered to be a network in decline, but has again started to pick up in interest, engagement and activity since 2017. This was helped in part by a generous investment by prominent figures like Mark Cuban, buying shares of Twitter after it started "Getting its act together" (*Source: http://www.businessinsider.com/mark-cuban-buying-twitter-stock-2017-5*) putting faith in the platform after the purchase of Magic Pony, an Ai company with powerful technology now owned by Twitter. Things have changed since then having Twitter pivot into a top news source in social media, surpassing the once reigning Reddit. Nowadays Twitter is more profitable than ever with effective ads that are not considered intrusive.

You may be wondering why is it, Twitter keeps coming back into relevance. That is because not only does it have a very solid user base that rivals the entire population of the United States, it has also, since its inception been in the interest of several powerful organizations, parties and individuals to keep it a valid and viable platform. It is no secret that Twitter was originally funded by the CIA, that it is still the first to break news with its realtime micro-blogging structure and is relied on by millions of people as a trusted source for genuine journalism. Whether it be the FBI, public figures, celebrities, politicians, major brands, marketers, small businesses, artists or producers, Twitter has, time and again proved itself to be a viable platform to accomplish anything you could ever dream of yet only a minuscule percentage of people taking advantage of the platform actually know how to accomplish it, while it continues to change. A lot of awareness for recent protests in Bolivia, Hong Kong, Chile and more were due in part to the many breaking posts from independent, mainstream and civilian journalism over those events on Twitter. Even without achieving continuous growth in new users, Twitter's ability to profit has only shot up. Only a fraction of those top profiles you see seem to actually know how to leverage Twitter for real business, fundraising, campaigning, selling or making a difference, regardless of how successful one appears.

In this book you will learn that when it comes to social media, there are three completely separate learning curves you will need to master in order to make the most of it; network expansion, content strategy and relationship building.

Three Disciplines

1. *Network expansion*, to increase the scope of your reach and be seen by a growing number of people.

2. *Content strategy*, to increase the amount of engagement any of your tweets or posts get to really

establish your legitimacy and status (the point even big names often fail upon!).

3. Relationship Building, to connect with your audience one-by-one to not only learn what makes your people tick, but to build long-lasting bonds which can be invaluable to anything you could ever want to achieve.

If you are reading this book, chances are you already believe in the viability of Twitter as a legitimate platform, but with the explosion of other social media channels like Facebook, Instagram and Snapchat, it is safe to assume there may still be a lot of skepticism in 2020. For this reason I will provide you some facts, courtesy of Hootsuite and eMarketer to back up those claims:

- **There are approximately 145 million monetizable daily active users**

- **Twitter's US user base is predicted grow 0.3% in 2020**

- **30 million (or 20%) of its user base are American**

- *92% of Americans know of Twitter (even if they don't use it)*

- *22% of adults in the US use Twitter*

- *44% of US 18 to 24 year-olds use Twitter*

- *US-based users are younger, wealthier & educated*

- *American Twitter users are more likely to be Democrat than average Americans*

- *The most prolific 10% of US Tweeters are women in politics*

- *80% of US Tweets come from 10% of the users*

- *Most active Twitter users are likely to have about 20X the amount of followers than average users*

- *12% of Americans get their news from Twitter*

- *13% of US users keep their accounts private*

- *Twitter's site referral traffic up 6% year-after-year*

- *Twitter users are more likely to like brands that are inclusive and transparent*

- *Twitter ad engagement is up 23%*

- *Twitter Ads are 50% cheaper when videos are included after calculating cost per engagement*

- *Twitter users spend 26% more time with ads than other social media users*

- *Twitter users spend another 24% more time with ads when they are from trusted content creators*

- *25% of Twitter's most prolific users employ scheduler software*

- *Tweets with hashtags get 100% more engagement*

- *People watch 2 billion videos on Twitter a day*

- *Watching video is #3 reason people use Twitter (after news and photos)*

- *Tweets with videos get 10X more engagement*

- *93% of video views on Twitter happen on mobile*

- *Videos get more retweets*

- ***Promoted accounts help Twitter users connect with brands***

- ***Twitter can influence buying decisions***

Moreover Twitter is no longer the extremely minimalistic platform it once was when it first launched in March, 2006, it now is full-featured, rivalling most major social media platforms. With the introduction of a 280 character limit in November of 2017, doubling the original 140 characters, Twitter has been refreshed with a whole new life, reinvigorating its status as a relevant platform that keeps up to date while keeping its loyal user base. Unlike its early days which literally only featured the ability to Tweet very short text based posts, I had been fortunate enough, since joining the platform in 2009 to watch it as it developed into a platform which once required users to copy and paste URLs into their browser to access suggested sites, to now including automatically clickable hyperlinks with auto-generating website previews for compatible sites much like Facebook or LinkedIn (and now many more). Furthermore it used to be impossible to natively display images in Twitter, most relying on 3rd-party websites and services to host images to link to from Twitter. How times have changed! Not only does Twitter now host its own images natively in your Tweets, much like Instagram or Facebook, it also has a host of features that at times even give it an edge against other platforms. Though Facebook was once the social media juggernaut that has since the beginning been first to implement the most features, the sheer scope of what is possible on the platform can be quite daunting. That level of complexity over time has shown Twitter to be a thorn in the side of Facebook, which explains their procurement of Instagram, their greatest likely competitor, much more minimalistic and less stressful to learn than Mark Zuckerberg's mammoth beast. As it becomes more of a hub for other social media, group-based content and direct messaging, its place has changed. Regardless of Facebook's famous targeting ability in paid ads; for free, Twitter's analytics availability is incredibly powerful and unmatched by most others, you do not have to be a marketing expert like you do on Facebook to really make quick and practical use of the information that lets you constantly know what makes your audience tick.

Twitter, unlike Facebook, is still a much simpler, cleaner and easy-to-learn platform, yet has advanced in some regards beyond the limitations and features of Instagram. That is why Twitter is the perfect platform for sub-cultures and niches, and the proof is in the pudding; if you learn the content that is in this book you too will be able to recognize when witnessing the thriving communities in a massive range of interests and industries better immersed for yourself. With powerful tools now built-in like polls, live streams (via Twitter's acquisition of Periscope) and embedded video clips, which are now a powerful medium for video advertising and driving traffic to longer form videos off site, Twitter has become a force to be reckoned with again and again reinventing itself with the times in our current social media era. So setup your concentration, relaxation or focus music, grab your cup of tea or coffee, or do whatever it is you do when you are ready to learn something life changing from a book, take a deep breath and be ready to take it all in.

Are you ready to go from zero (or wherever you are) on Twitter - potentially struggling to get anywhere on the platform - to becoming a more legitimate influencer? Are you ready to take your account - no matter what status it currently is - to a whole new level? Are you ready to learn what I had to learn for myself through my own blood, sweat and tears, research and implementation that it took to be higher than the Top 1% of accounts in Twitter-verse; to become a genuine social media influencer, even rivalling major names and brands? Then read on.

This may sound too good to be true, but I, like you today, started my Twitter journey by learning from a simple book about how to grow my account on Twitter. It was a free book available as a bonus to an in-depth course on LinkedIn by Lewis Howes, which I read from front to back after completing and applying every last lesson of the course to my LinkedIn. It was suggested by Howes as a great way to drive traffic to my LinkedIn profile, and indeed that strategy worked, but that book only focused on growing a following and is now outdated by about 8 years since I read it. The book you are currently reading however goes far beyond just growing your following, which ultimately may not be as important as you think, to even teach you the secrets current Twitter influencer wannabes and even established names would pay a pretty penny to learn and apply. It is up to date with everything Twitter has to offer today, and as you know Twitter is a much more sophisticated platform now than it was then. Not only will you learn how to grow your audience, as the title of the book suggests, you will also learn free marketing strategies to engage your audience and how you can turn a potentially distracting social media pastime into a full-fledged viable business.

"To disrupt your market, you can't listen to naysayers."
- Guy Kawasaki

I have checked every single major Twitter book on the market, and no one else covers mastery of the platform quite like me. Many of the books make large claims, some right in the title that you can achieve things like growing your account to 100,000 real followers in 6 months, but what it does not make clear until you actually read the entire book that such a thing cannot be achieved alone by an individual and certainly not for free.

Everything I teach you in this book is my first-hand experience as a completely solo individual building my Twitter account, particularly over the last year and a half where I was able to take it from over 10,000 followers to now nearly 50,000 followers strong, even without having to follow anywhere close to the amount of people that follow me (which you may note as a common phenomena among many major influencer accounts on Twitter) and moreover if you do happen to have the resources and team to apply these concepts I have applied as a *commando assassin*, so to speak, it is an incredibly powerful set of tools to expand and conquer your digital landscape through the medium without having to use many cheap tricks, illegitimate practices, nor breaking Twitter's rules while creating a solid network reach of *tens of thousands+* of real, living breathing people who actually care about you, and even share your deepest interests. Sound good? If so, hold tight, you are in for a wild ride!

Growing A Following

When it comes to building a business with your social media account, there is something that I keep stressing. The three major disciplines that need to be mastered that are correlated but not causing one another, mentioned in the preface. Many assume that if you have one, you will have all, and although such a principle may apply at an esoteric level, that goes beyond the scope or theme of this book. In reality though one of those disciplines can definitely benefit the other, one can never replace or do the job of the other. For instance, this first section is all about growing your following, expanding your network and increasing your reach using Twitter's built-in tools and the occasional free 3rd-party add-on optionally to make things a little bit easier and less time-consuming, however that does not mean if you master this one discipline alone, getting 10 thousand or more followers much will engage with your shared content. Let alone them engaging when it is by you at first. As you learn about how to grow your following here from multiple angles keep in mind the cold, hard, truth that others may fail to realize or mention; growing your following does not equate building your community nor increasing your sales!

Do not fret though because this book is the ultimate advanced Twitter guide, developed to give you the platforms and tools to do business and sales therein.

Furthermore sales are difficult to scale without some form of real engagement, and that is why this book covers all. Though I could start with the sales portion, without the engagement you would eventually hit a wall and not know what to do when you really wanted to multiply the revenues you are generating in your next sales cycle. In that case the engagement factor - achieved through content strategy - becomes vital. Although you could master engagement within a smaller reach and following, it may be more challenging for consistent traffic (though you may still have viral content with a tiny following) but if you focus and dial it in, it can be a quality over quantity situation which may be of more value than a large following that are not in your niche.

That is why it is safe to say that expanding your reach in your niche and increasing your targeted relationships is the best way for you to start. The reason for starting with followers is because it is less challenging nor requires the same level of courage as the other two disciplines, it is a great place to get your feet wet in what can be done within a social media channel, as well as the perfect training ground for developing habits in becoming consistent with employing social media as a serious tool for your life and business. First things will be first and we will go from the basics to the more advanced principles. Every chapter will follow that format, so that you can really ease into it achieving what Gary Keller refers to as the "Domino Effect," beginning with the one thing that you can do immediately that if you keep going and keep advancing with your learning will result in a chain-reaction that has the more challenging and advanced principles seem as easy as the most basic and simple ones due to the gradual process, a step-by-step process that leads you there. It is like the contortionist who can do a full splits with her legs or literally bend over backwards to the point her head is able to peak through her legs, not from the front but the back; it all started with the most basic stretches, perhaps not even being able to touch the toes, but with continual practice of the basics the perception of the challenge at the next level will only feel as difficult as the last challenge was before it was mastered. So many people want to touch their toes on day one, but have not taken the time to stretch through the tensions at the most basic level and so attempting to do so is painful and can break ones morale which is why most give up and cannot even get that far! Therefore in order for you not to feel it is an order beyond the magnitude of what you can achieve, we begin with the simplest and easiest discipline which will later serve as the foundation for everything else.

Setting Up Your Account

First things first, whether you already have a Twitter profile set up or it is your first time setting one up, let us not bore you with the basic details to set one up in terms of signing up with your email and so on but instead focus on the pointers that you need to ensure you pay attention to ascertain an account that people will not feel reluctant to follow so we shall focus on those.

Be Thorough

It really sickens me at this point, and I hope it causes no offence, but it is the truth; accounts that lack the most basic things such as a profile picture or a bio really are a red flag to "STAY AWAY" from such accounts. If that is you, do not fret, it is easily changeable! You might tell me "But I'm ugly" or "I do not have a quality head shot" or many other such excuses, but in reality you can even use a company logo if you are using a brand account. If you do not even have a company logo I wonder why you are reading a book about running a business? I would think that at the very least you have some brand you are promoting or there is no way for potential leads to differentiate you from anyone else. You would be surprised though what a relatable face regardless of taste can do for connecting with people where a logo may need more promotion first. "Beauty is in the eye of the beholder" after all. Whether it be a pro headshot for your personal brand or even a nicely taken selfie, a professional company logo or even clear, legible text that says the name of your company or your brand, just do not leave it blank! Also do not use someone else's picture or a picture of a brand you like. Also do not use any image you think looks cool or anything along those lines if it is not clearly representing your brand. I know this sounds extremely basic and is not meant to be condescending but there are an incredible amount of accounts, probably the majority of accounts where the avatar does not clearly represent them nor their business, worse off some do not even bother to put up an avatar. If you are one of those people without an avatar and you are not willing to change that, I beg you to stop reading this book now and try something else! Then again you could always open up a second account. Otherwise this is not for you and you should not be wondering later "Why is no one following me?" If you have already done this or are willing to do it, read on.

The next thing is a cover image that also represents you, your company or brand clearly, this should not be the same as your avatar and generally I would avoid any people in your cover art unless it is highly meaningful, appropriate and high quality enough to not only look good but make you look better without being blown up and blurry. I have to emphasize this again, make sure the image you use is of high resolution enough that it will not get pixelated. Also make sure to pay attention to the dimensions of the image. It may be OK for the art to get cut off a bit due to the very wide and short dimensions you get to work with as long as it is crisp and you can position it in a way that looks intentional and not obviously cut off or distorted. I suggest a high resolution image of your logo made to fit the cover art area either by adding white space around it (note: the "white space" can be any colour, whatever matches the logo best) or by ensuring the design fits right into those dimensions.

Though I find having people in your cover art usually does not look good, there are exceptions like highly professional composited images by a graphic designer who really knows their stuff and can make it look like a professional banner. Personally, I prefer a clear logo as that is stark, clear and focused, but if you must, you can also take the pro wide bus advertisement (as if it was done by a top fashion magazine) or HQ banner approach, but once again, do not leave it blank! I know Twitter allows you to choose from a range of blank colours, but if I see that on an account the first word that comes to my mind is "lazy" and that is definitely not going to help you gain followers! Remember that your profile is like your business flyer, it is supposed to promote you and what you do, so if it looks unprofessional, that is the exact impression people will get.

You also need to make sure you put in a biography; avoid at all costs auto-generated bios you can get made with some sites for that online, though the layman may not know, any chance of being able to collaborate with influencers will be damaged by doing that. The reason is that influencers, at least from what I can see, can immediately tell if your bio is auto-generated. How can I tell? They all follow the exact same format and writing style and frankly the content tends to be random; you cannot fake it! So go ahead and put the one thing you do that provides value to others, and make sure you also include a link to your website or main professional social media page from another channel, preferably LinkedIn. I would say LinkedIn is the best choice as it does an excellent job of complimenting Twitter rather than competing like Facebook and gives more incentive for people to click than a Youtube account which tends to be more load-heavy than a more text-oriented website. Instagram is also a close competitor, but I cannot tell you how many people just want to use their Twitter to redirect to their Instagram, this would have made sense 6 years ago when Twitter did not have the ability to post images directly in a Tweet, but since that has already been available for several years, using Instagram (or flickr or Pinterest or any other image gallery app) only tells the person looking at your profile that you want to take them off Twitter to another social media site which can be bad news if him or her expects you to be bringing value natively within the app currently being used. Not to say there is no time or place to promote other networks, as you may put together from the information in this book, but it is not the best way to go about maximizing your account most of the time.

If you do multiple things, make it clear, intentional and organized and always go back to how you are helping the person reading. For example mine once said "Creative at heart with a strong technical background, now focused on business to help you!" As I am one who does many things, I found a way to *wrap it in a story* to make it one thought instead of three and five, finally with the punch-line that it is to "help you!" You do not have to follow this exact format, you could put something like "Specializing in graphic design to take your brand to the next level" if you mainly centralize around one discipline or "Artist, writer and performer of works to help bring a smile to your face." There is no hard rules on the format, but the point is being honest, clear and about helping whomever happens to be reading it. Sometimes you have a lot to say and want to stay within the character limit, so be clear and direct to the point like my current bio "Design, Development & Programming in Marketing & Entertainment" stating what I do on the left with what industries I do it in on the right, leaving room for links to my LinkedIn profile and SecureCheckout.Live e-shop.

Besides the already mentioned importance of linking to a page right from the bio (your website or LinkedIn are recommended), there is also a field Twitter provides especially for linking to your own site. You might think it is an opportunity to promote or push a second website but ironically that is not effective and only splits the focus on what you are trying to promote, instead put one of the exact same website addresses there as you did in your bio. This seems redundant, but later in this book, where we talk about driving traffic I will explain why it works.

You may not want to put your birth date and ultimately it is not that large of an issue unless you look underage in your avatar and are trying to promote yourself as someone fit for tasks or responsibilities exclusive to adults and want to ensure that your age is clear. Do not lie or fib here however as it could end up biting you back in the ass later! If you really are underage, go ahead and put your real birthdate, it will actually be an advantage, not for trying to do anything illegal for your age limit, but by following the content of this book at such a young age it will be highly impressive to visitors and increase the likelihood they follow you. Otherwise if you are one of those people who is embarrassed or afraid to share your age because you are older, you can keep it clear, but as the title of this section states "Be Thorough," the more you fill in properly and accurately the better, so it may not make a huge difference but sometimes it is the smallest things that have the most impact so choose at your own discretion.

Finally a big one, your location; do not leave this blank or vague! Do not put some non-existent or made-up location! Do not be afraid to put your real location. This will really provide legitimacy, trust and authenticity to your accounts. Too many accounts, sometimes even pretty established ones do this wrong and put "Worldwide" or something like "On a space asteroid" or some other nonsense like that. Everyone is living on the earth (I think); that gives the reader no valuable information. While putting something imaginary or fake just has the reader think you have trust issues which may lead them to believe you should not be trusted. Therefore be thorough, be clear, be honest and consider the perspective of those visiting.

Followers, The First 1k

> *"You only need 1,000 true fans."*
> - Kevin Kelly

At one point the initial follow limit set by Twitter was 2,000 before requiring to be followed back in order to keep following but now it appears this number has gone to 5,000. In some ways this makes those armed with the information in a book like this at an advantage to myself years ago when I started working on my Twitter growth, however with recent changes there are now disadvantages in terms of the speed you can grow an account by following new people to about 40% of what it once was. At the same time this new rule makes it easier for those less informed about how to use Twitter to get trapped into a situation where they are following nearly 5,000 people with as little as a handful following back, something which used to happen often. This is no fun because if you want to apply what is being taught here, it will require several hours of extra work to take you out of that situation. Though I will go more into why, in a moment, the first thing you should do is not follow people, but make sure you have an on-brand avatar, clear or comical Twitter name, an informative and welcoming bio description that makes it clear what kind of person you are, making it easier to attract those same or complimentary type of people to follow you, but if you do follow, make sure it is people in your interest and niche.

As mentioned the limit used to be 2,000 followers when I first got on the platform, but now it has been raised to 5,000, meaning it is easier to have a follower base of around 5,000 targeted people than ever since that change in 2015. I remember being very happy with about 2,000 followers in 2013, nowadays new users have the luxury of making that 5,000 without a huge amount of effort over a longer time. However if, like me, you are highly observant to the status of most Twitter accounts, you will see a very common pattern and phenomena. You will see accounts that can never get passed that 5,000 mark. I actually did not even know about the change in limit, I simply saw the pattern that now many were not getting stuck at 2,000 but 5,000. After a quick Google search, I found out the limit was indeed changed, but the problem of many being unable to grow past that limit, stayed the same. That is because most of them do not know how to get passed that barrier but that is one of the major purposes of this book, to ensure you not only overcome the initial Twitter limit, but that you do not stop growing your Twitter every single day.

Growing A Network

So you have signed up for Twitter, created your password and now Twitter is suggesting to you people to follow. Many of us, myself included, at this point follow for the "Celeb Trap" as I call it, trying to find and follow every celebrity's official Twitter account that you love. Although there are rare cases where a celebrity may follow you back, with a brand new account and no status the likelihood of that is extremely low, and not worth filling up your precious follow limits set upon you by Twitter. If you follow that path, before you know it you will reach your follow limit while having little to no people following you back, essentially being a large waste of time. If these celebrities Tweet anything trendy, chances are thousands, tens of thousands, hundreds of thousands or more people will retweet what that celebrity has said, making it likely you will still see their Tweets indirectly. Otherwise you can always check that celebrity's Twitter account for their feeds, this ensures you can see every single thing they post without following them. Instead of following celebrities or certified accounts at the beginning which are unlikely to follow back, I suggest pulling from your email list or other connections or contacts you have, if any, and following the followers of those connections before even considering following a celebrity or influencer on Twitter. If you have no connections of your own,

Tweetdeck has a powerful search feature that you can use to find that celebrity's tweet, or more importantly find those among Twitter's 300 million user base that are likely to follow back, otherwise add them to a list unless you are a diehard fan and will follow them even if they ignore you. Your avatar, name, bio descriptions and activity on your account go a long way in your potential followers deciding to follow you back, because you have to build your way up from scratch.

Private Followers

As you learn the best way to go about following people in order to build your profile, you will come across "protected accounts" which require approval from the user before you can follow them. This, in my experience does not really change whether or not they will follow you back. Interestingly enough, after following multiple protected accounts, I have found that some will even follow you back without approving you following them or vice-versa. In most cases however, those that allow you to follow them will follow back, but is generally not an issue to be too concerned with. For the purpose of this book I would completely recommend against your setting your own account to protected, unless it is a separate account from the one you will use to grow your Twitter status, unless you are really dedicated to experimenting with that feature.

Keywords & Benchmarks

Now that you have found out what is important in setting up your account, how to avoid the celeb trap and any confusion about protected accounts has been cleared up, we can get into who you should actually follow. This will be based on a specific target you have in mind. The avatar you choose, the name you choose for your account, your bio description and the kind of activity you engage in will form an image of the kind of account or channel you have. Those that choose to follow you or not will base it on how you present yourself that way. Thus for the greatest likelihood of being followed back, one strategy that has proven effective again and again is to model the Twitter accounts of those that come closest to representing the same kind of culture or brand that you would like to be associated with. If you feel you need to do some updates to the kind of keywords you use in your profile and the kind of image you present, those users who you wish to become like provide the best inspiration. Furthermore their followers are more likely to follow you back if they feel you represent more or less the same kind of things in your own unique way as those they already follow.

Targeting Your Niche

Although you may have read some other books about growing a following on Twitter that told you to just find the followers of an influencer and just follow everyone of their followers, wait 24 hours (since that is within Twitter's rules and limits) and then unfollow the ones that did not follow you back, a very powerful and simple technique which can grow a following steadily day-to-day when done with discipline; many seem to fail to mention how you can ensure those people are actually within your interests and even less have I seen them talk about location. This is a good strategy, but only if you are selective and careful with who you are choosing to follow. Of course it is beneficial to just go ahead and follow everyone, playing the numbers game, assuming you have set your account up nicely in the last section, you should expect at least a 10-15% followback rate at the beginning (for a general audience, potentially less at first for an elite niche), but that is only for increasing a number, for it to have more value there are some pointers I am going to share with you here to not only increase that followback percentage but also ensure you are not just increasing the quantity of your followers but that you also ascertain the quality just as much if not more.

Of course depending how well you target who you follow against your profile you could achieve a higher follow back rate, all the way up to 50%, sometimes even more, and today into 2020, so far that may happen more often, but in most cases, especially while your profile is still new, and does not have many followers yet, it is more challenging to get that followback rate at the start. Now of course there are some exceptions, for example parody accounts of famous celebrities, very attractive females that post authentic pictures of themselves, and if you happen to already be very well-known, you are much more likely to get a high followback rate. However this book was not meant for those that are likely to have some kind of advantage on the platform, but rather for anyone who wants to increase their brand awareness on the platform. Though of course it can only help those that are already in that kind of status as well. That means regardless of how well you are known, how attractive you are and even if it is an authentic account, referring to nothing known or famous, assuming you set it up to reflect who you are in the most approachable way, you can expect at least a 10-15% followback rate, if not more. This average will thankfully increase however as you get better at targeting, choosing who you follow, and your account gets more influential. In a very strange way, this makes Twitter (and other social media) work like an idle farming mobile app, but fortunately much more potentially meaningful to your real life and relationships as long as you follow through.

Also if you want to target local people in particular, a great way to start is to use Tweetdeck with relevant keywords colloquial to those locales. This should be available in there, along with other such advanced features accessible with your regular Twitter account too. If you setup your account properly with your actual location, this will work to find the trends in your area by default to have some preliminary content to discuss. You can also change your location to target other specific locations by default, or pick a different one for trends alone.

<u>You can immediately qualify people with this criteria:</u>

1. Has the person posted recently?

2. Does his or her profile look decent?

3. Does his or her profile look authentic?

4. Does his or her profile look decent?

5. Is this person within your target interest or niche?

That list is also a self-evident guide on how your profile should seem to others. From there you can decide if that person is worth following and most importantly reaching out to by liking, retweeting, or tweeting at to engage the person. This could be used for finding a mate even instead of Tinder, but that is a whole other story. Otherwise it is great for finding any kind of prospect for any purpose and you are then qualifying on many levels in advance with the only major caveat being a lower likelihood of response from the get-go but considering you following the above and having a nice profile and also being local, there is a good chance that this could be a very quality potential relationship. That is a strategy for extreme targeting, putting quality over quantity to the Nth degree. To de-stress those worrying, it should be mentioned that Twitter has anti-scam features built-in to automate the catching and reduction of scams.

1st Round Of Unfollowing

Now you may have started doing the math, calculating that "If I follow 5,000 people on Twitter and I'm sure to get about 10% following me back, that's only 500 people!" This is absolutely correct. Instead of going and following 5,000 people first however I recommend only following 400 to start, waiting 24 hours and then going through and unfollowing all of those that are not following you back. To do this you need to go into the list of who you are currently following and see which accounts include the little note "Follows You" and which ones do not. For everyone you followed, after more than 24 hours that does not have any indication that they followed you back, you can go ahead and unfollow them. Do this for every single one you find. This should not be too hard at this point, although you could use an app to find them and list some of them for you, commun.it - and other such sites - early on, this is not as necessary because the amount you follow will be small enough to be manageable at that point. By only following 400 at a time, after every 24 hours, and unfollowing those that did not follow you back, you are developing the right kind of habits, following the process that you will consistently need to follow even after you have already reached beyond 5,000 followers. This way you are less likely to feel a slowdown or halt in progress when that limit is reached, ideally it will not even feel like you hit a limit at all, and you will simply be able to keep going as long as you follow that daily strategy. Do make sure you never start unfollowing those you have followed in less than 24 hours, because if you do that with too many accounts, you risk going against Twitter's rules and getting your account shut down. You may also be concerned that 24 hours is not enough time to give people to follow you back, if that is the case it may be worth waiting up to 72 hours for some to notice. This however is not an issue, because you will always have the opportunity to follow those same accounts later if you come across them, giving them another chance to follow you back then, though this may annoy some but as the old saying goes, *"Those that mind don't matter while those that matter don't mind."* You need to find the people that really love you! Not just the ones that accept you. I know as most of what I am telling you has been learnt from my own mistakes.

You may notice Twitter only allowing you to follow 50 at a time, but you can simply wait about 60-90 seconds when you hit that temporary limit for it to be lifted for another 50 accounts. This goes on until you reach a total of 400. That limit is lifted again about 12-24 hours later.

Twitter's Search Feature

Whether you already have a following consisting of people already from your network that Twitter allowed you to find based on your email or not, the search tool is invaluable for finding people in your niche. Adding to the network of individuals that will be beneficial to your mission, message or objectives. Though it was more robust on site and in-app in the past, it has become more limited without going ahead to the Tweetdeck to do your search business. Simply type in keywords that relate to your niche in a search and check not only the posts but the people. When clicking on a person's profile, check their location, keep doing this until you find the one that clearly is in your niche based on their bio and posts with their stated location being the one for which you are looking. Once you have found that person, ideally someone with several hundred to a couple thousand followers, I would not recommend those that have much more than that usually. Quickly scroll through their followers accounts and scan for their quality. If it looks like a good portion of them have failed to meet the standards laid out in the previous section for setting up accounts, do not follow them.

Even though they may seem to be connected to your niche and location, not coming close to those standards set for setting up an account you have now learned is a sign of low quality followers that you probably do not even want. Once you find that profile with the interests and niche within the location of your choice, and you can see the majority of their following coming much closer or even matching those guidelines for properly setting up an account, then it is a good idea to follow as many of them as possible. Twitter will only allow you to follow 400 at a time, but this does not have to come from one account, it could be from finding several accounts that match your desired targeting that each only have a few 100s of followers, which is sometimes recommended since the likelihood of them being higher quality increases in such cases, however I have found that some with several

1000s can still be of very high quality, so make sure to scroll through them for the quality before doing any kind of mass follow strategy.

If you know what you are looking for, it should not take you more than 10-20 minutes to find them, and with 3rd-party tools like the free "Follow all" extension for Google Chrome (or an equivalent free app, tool or extension, letting you follow 50 at a time, until you refresh the page and find those yet to be followed on page), it is also easy to follow them all quite quickly, but if you are not on desktop or do not use Chrome, do not fret you can just go ahead and do it manually, though 400 people a day or so might seem like a lot of work, especially manually, it is exactly how I started and if you do so without any distractions nor multitasking it will work for you too. In certain cases Twitter may say you cannot follow any more after only following 20-50 people, but simply stop and wait about 60-90 seconds before continuing. Playing back "focus" or "concentration" music in the background from Youtube, your favourite streaming service or any ritual that helps you focus makes this much easier to handle. These days I also recommend listening to audio books or courses while doing it as a concentration strategy so that you can study and work at the same time. You should be able to follow 400 in less than 30 minutes if you do nothing else. I do warn however that if you are distracted and try to do other things at the same time, answer emails, check other social media or any other tasks at the same time, that 30 minutes could stretch out into several hours, even the whole entire day if you are not careful. I suspect this is the reason why, those that may even know some version of this strategy give up and fail to build a following because of their unfocused approach making it seem they need to spend 8 hours a day to achieve it when everything from start to end, especially when you get habituated, even without the help of a 3rd-party extension should only really take 30-60 minutes max, if you ensure that time is dedicated and focused as mentioned. After 24 hours has passed you can go through your list of followers and simply unfollow the ones who never followed you back, you can play with this strategy and wait 48 or 72 hours instead, but my experience is that the 24 hours is usually enough time to find out mostly who would follow you back based on your profile. Though you can go by how frequently they post, RT or like for an estimate of that specific account's activity.

Also of note is the time of the day when you follow people, that is because the moment someone is followed, he or she will receive a notification - assuming the phone is on - but if it is at a time of the day when the person is asleep or very busy, the likelihood of that person following you back drops simply due to their not noticing you followed in the first place. Though the person also received an email notifying of the follow, there is no guarantee the person will check nor that it was not buried by another bunch of emails by the time he or she checks. That is why following people early before work time, during lunch breaks, after work or in the evening in their time zones tends to be the most likely time they will see the notification of your follow in real time, increasing the likelihood he or she will take enough notice to follow you back.

Though it will add extra time, you can also, after following a large number of accounts, look at your timeline or go to each account individually and like their posts, the more the better. This is recommended to increase the likelihood of following back, but in my experience I have not found the increase in followback rate by doing this that much higher, the truth is people seem to care most about your profile, since that is the quickest and easiest way to judge, so you can use this 'like' technique and it may work to increase your following quicker, but the added time and effort may not be worth the minimal return, so simply like what you like! I prefer to just go about liking naturally, literally liking what I like and usually mainly within those already following me back, because it is not just a matter of getting people to follow you, but to build relationships, however we will get more into that later on in the book. Up next are some strategies that will increase your followback rate without having to use that liking strategy you may have heard suggested on certain websites online.

Building Your Network

Now that you have setup an attractive profile, and have begun building up your network, you can start implementing more advanced strategies for growing your following. Now that you have a pool of followers to work with you can start expanding through the network you have already began to build. From here on out, although you can still use Twitter's search function via keywords or hashtags to find more users in your niche, an even better method at this point is to find new followers from within the followers you already have. The reason for this is because it dramatically increases your followback rate, in most cases, assuming you do a proper scan of the following and the quality as well as the target niche matches. I have experienced at the beginning jumping from that average of 10-15% follow back when first establishing my network to 30-40% with this simple strategy alone, and those numbers may be even better if it was today albeit within a smaller amount of accounts at a time. Unless you run out of quality users in your network to do this with (which is usually unlikely) or you are trying to expand your network into other niches than you have already been targeting, from now on, following the followers of followers already following you is the best way to go most of the time.

From here you might want to consider sending out "shout-outs," participating in trending hashtags, as well as Twitter standard weekly practices like #MondayMotivation, #TuesdayThoughts, #WednesdayWisdom, #ThrowbackThursday and #FollowFriday to increase your reach to new people outside and inside your network, if not a first degree connection. Twitter Trends are based on the location that you set for trends, but it is better not to use the trending hashtag or word unless you have something highly entertaining, valuable or apt to contribute to it. I also suggest trying the 3rd-party site SocialRank, a website that helps you find out more about your followers. This is a fairly easy to use site that has its best features free and I recommend it if you are to take your blossoming Twitter business seriously. It is a great way to find out who is who in your network and to more easily connect with them by interests. It is also something your followers will appreciate as doing so only helps you mention those who have interest in your content. Even beyond those you can follow up with in your notifications, it is a great way to help you prepare Twitter Lists. SocialRank also has a powerful "Best Follower" filter to see who are really the closest connections at the current time. You can update the accuracy against your current following by using the refresh button at the top of the page.

Otherwise there are multiple free services out there to learn about your community, I recommend in particular other than the aforementioned SocialRank which is a go-to, Tweepsmap is an amazing website that has awesome free features as well that are substantial enough to get you in-the-know of what kind of people are in your community. Another interesting free service is Empire.Kred which offers missions and presents you as a virtual stock where shares can be bought by points within the system to raise your status, but it really seems to be best used for exposure to mostly older crowds who play that fantasy social media game. The missions when executed are also a way to increase your reach and build your network. There is also SocialBearing which measures your overall tweet data online building word clouds and providing filter options for your tweets. That is only a handful of the available services and tools, but are the ones I recommend most and have found most useful, though there are in fact many others and worth Googling to your specific need. Twitter's own analytics service "Twitter Analytics" is also completely free and is the bread and butter for analytics to know who your audience really is which should not be forgotten even if it may seem obvious. Otherwise it cannot be stressed enough that power users can also make use of Twitter's own TweetDeck for more full-fledged features when using Twitter to make it easier to do more, but I would only save that for when you are doing some Twitter searches where you need to find something specific you tweeted for a self-retweet, are attempting intensive campaigns, or are in need of such advanced tools when collaborating with other Twitter users.

Besides the above there are also ways to see how you rank in the Twitter-verse with SocialBlade also tracking your influence and statistics. A good compliment to that is SocialBearing which tends to give slightly different statistics than Twitter Analytics, this is due to each system using a different percentage of data to estimate overall facts about your account than each other while focusing on different metrics to measure, employing different algorithms that have results vary. If you go ahead and look at the status of your network reach and influence from these multiple services, first and third party, you can approximate an overall reality of where you and your network really stands. These systems are also continually improving everyday so make sure to look more often than once before judging any truths about what is going on with the standing of your account and connections, better understanding your audience and position.

Driving Traffic

As mentioned when setting up your account, you want to put the website link you are trying to drive traffic to, not only in the website field of your profile but just as well in your bio. However to increase the likelihood of driving traffic even further, post a Tweet with your website address included, hopefully with relatable or humorous text to accompany it as well as an image that is also just as appealing as the text, ideally with overlaid text of its own, the format of a meme, since that is the most engaging format. The text in the tweet does not have to match the text in the meme or a fun video, and in fact my experiments have found that when the text and media do not exactly match but correlate you get higher engagement percentages. Finally for those you want passive traffic use the "pin tweet" feature to infinitely have this tweet at the top of your posts so that no matter what you tweeted recently, when new potential followers come to visit your profile they will see the pinned tweet first, and since it includes that link to your website, it increases the likelihood of driving traffic to your intended location.

Furthermore to be able to drive more traffic beyond all of the above will be with your content strategy. If you post a piece of content from your website or LinkedIn (where you can publish blog posts to share) and tweet it, ensure that the automatically generated image preview is coming up with the link. If not save or copy that image and paste it with the Tweet when you share. This tends to not be as much of an issue nowadays but better to not be lazy. Ideally each post in fact follows the exact same *poster* or video approach described in the preceding paragraph, this ensures you get more engagement with each post from your site, increasing the likelihood of link clicks, further generating traffic. Entertainment and value are key. Beyond this you can take any of those Tweets and setup a paid campaign with Twitter Ads, though it is not free and requires a lot of setup, it is a legit way to increase traffic, but otherwise if you do not want to go through the hassle of setting up the promotional campaign what you can do for free, since a couple of years ago is retweet yourself. You can go even further and retweet yourself multiple times, as many times as you want. Furthermore when appropriate, like it is someone in the niche of the content, you can embed Tweets in a direct message (DM) as well by DMing the Tweet's link.

Some warnings about retweeting yourself should be mentioned before you do so. First of all, ensure that the tweet is getting proper engagement, do that by going to Twitter Analytics and checking the engagement percentile or clicking the analytics mini-graph button. Anything at 1.0% or higher is fair game for retweeting yourself and multiple times (until that number drops). You do not have to use that number, you can use a higher standard, but it is the perfect sweet spot between average (<0.5%) and top level engagement (5.0%+) which is difficult to achieve on any level of consistency. I will help you to achieve that however in later chapters, but in most cases, my standard is 1.0%+, two or more times the average engagement. Moreover you do not even have to go to the Twitter Analytics website anymore to track a Tweet's engagement, you can now simply click on the vertical bar graph icon that appears since recent times at the bottom-right corner of your own Tweet. It will list all the activity on the Tweet but the two numbers you need to pay attention to are the *impressions* number and the *engagements* number. From there you can do a simple calculation to find out the engagement percentage.

For example 200 impressions and 1 engagement is 0.5% engagement or 300 impressions and 6 engagements is equal to 2.0%. Back to the warnings I mentioned above, if you retweet yourself more than once Twitter can sometimes be difficult. What happens is if you are doing this on a mobile device and you want to retweet yourself more than once, first you have to unretweet yourself causing the tweet to go back to where it was originally Tweeted in your timeline, burying the Tweet and time consuming to scroll down to find again. So when on mobile first click on the tweet itself so you can unretweet it without it disappearing from your view, otherwise use Tweetdeck, search the tweet, unretweet and retweet from there since that issue there does not exist. If you are doing it on desktop that problem does not occur but another one does, where if you click directly on a tweet then attempt at a retweet, it may fail with an error message "Sorry that Tweet has been deleted," but worry not, it is wrong; you just need to refresh the page, better yet open the tweet in a new tab next time. You should be able to avoid that glitch.

All of the above when done correctly and consistently will continuously drive traffic to your website. As I said you may need to experiment to see what gets you higher engagement, but all you need is a handful of Tweets that are consistently engaging above 1.0% and you can retweet them again and again as often as you like while they still engage, though be considerate of those you tagged in a tweet as they may be notified when you do unless they mute that conversation.

With the reliability of doing the above consistently, when any one piece of content or your commentary on a hot topic tweeted becomes a hit, that one piece will become a traffic driver to your brand by itself, leading people to pay attention to your daily efforts.

Branding

Whether it be on traditional mass media, the book cover, the newspaper or magazine ad, the Radio spot, the TV commercial, the billboard, flyer or business card… just as well as face-to-face communications; branding is incredibly important. As you may be able to guess in emails, forums, blogs, messaging apps, teleconferencing apps, online adverts, funnels, videos and social media, branding remains just as much an incredibly powerful centralizing anchor to your sales, marketing and business. This is not just a tool to be utilized to improve your results, it is a completely inescapable reality of everything you do, meaning that if you pay no attention to branding, you are still branding yourself unintentionally as someone who has no concern for branding. That is why it is best to be aware of it and ensure it is completely congruent with the vision, mission and culture of the platform you are growing, enriching and ameliorating. Whether you are a small niche, a business hub or a personal brand, the central focus should be the brand and everything else should revolve around it.

You may be wondering, "How does this apply to growing my Twitter?" This is applicable to growing your Twitter in that it is one thing to get new followers, but it is a whole other thing to keep them. If you are followed by several thousand people for instance who did so because of the brand that appealed to them when they first came across your account, and that was to change so drastically that it is as if you are a whole different business altogether than that point, do not be surprised, unless this new image is more appealing to those same individuals, that they will swiftly unfollow. This is not to say you cannot keep developing your brand nor that you can never change how your present yourself, it is to say there needs to be a consistent core message, feeling and intention behind everything you do even as it develops and adapts with the times. Unless what you have done up to this point has been completely off-putting for more than 90% of people and proven to be a complete detractor from pretty much everybody, which is in fact rare, especially if you followed the proper profile setup tips brought up earlier in the book and you are not expecting your engagement to go up without a lot of time putting out content, when you go from one core message to a different one it sends your audience the message that you have no clue what you are doing. That can really hurt their confidence in you, having them no longer want to stick around which is why consistency keeps you relevant.

Therefore if you want to ensure that - not only your followers keep following - but you take yourself out of obscurity in the minds and hearts of your connections. You need to establish distinction, and remove the commoditizing of your business, so you really need to pay attention to your brand at all times on all accounts to ascertain you have a chance at lasting beyond a temporary phase. Moving towards sustainable exponential growth for the value of what you are realizing long term. This means that if you choose to be a personal brand with a face representing your organizations, keep that consistent, always keep it as a personal branding account, do not convert it into a logo or design after that has been established. As you may have concluded, it also works the other way around, the account that has a logo or design as its brand image should keep it along those lines consistently. Even if you update your logo or your avatar image, it should still be along the same kind of branding strategy, at least in terms of branding type, as it always has. If for some reason you have a strong personal brand but want to promote a company logo based brand, then the best strategy to stay consistent and congruent for your audience is to simply open up a separate account for that separate branding type. Each account can cross-promote each other by retweeting each other and considering the fact that, when you expand your network with the information presented in this book, your audiences may overlap but will not be the same, one account can in fact expand the reach of the other to new audiences for each brand.

This section will end with pointing out how a brand should be determined. A brand should not be determined simply by the results alone, work or content that you are delivering nor should it be hard set at any phase of presentation, instead it should revolve around the principles and values that the brand is attempting to represent. This way the brand can continue to stay fresh with updates to its manifestation while remaining true to the purpose and direction that has been intended all along. This can be reflected in improving the quality of the materials you post or how you present your business all the while staying true to your company or personal mission that is the compass for everything you put out there. Thus no one piece of content is isolated in a vacuum even if it is built to work natively. Nobody is perfect and neither is any company however, so there is a potential to update even your core values and pivot to a new trajectory, but that is only to be done when there is a valid reason and a genuine personal story. Time for transition should be made to inform the public of your self-reflection in the new path you are turning to, ensuring that it is for greater consistency over time, rather than an arbitrary change for the sake of change to appear busy. In most cases I would not recommend to go as far as changing the branding type. In any case it should stay true to your story.

Collaboration

When it comes to collaborating on Twitter, it is all about give and take. You cannot expect someone who is far ahead of you as an influencer to collaborate with you too easily, unless you have a solid platform for that person to promote him or her. This is all about reciprocation and when it works right, you are able to increase exposure for your own account while the other is able to do the same for theirs. Though I have done many collaborations with others at different levels online, it can be a challenge to pinpoint one thing that makes it all possible. Most of the time collaborations have happened when someone - either myself or the other person - has shown strong initiative and a strong reason to exchange resources. Just as you probably should not approach an influencer without having anything to offer them before asking to collaborate, you too should neither allow anyone, who is not doing anything notable to collaborate with you. After all you are either growing your brand or damaging it so choose wisely who you work with. That is not to say you should not feature those that look up to you, but that that person should be able to deliver value in their own right, ideally you are featuring someone ahead of you that you look up to.

The more consistently and the higher the quality of the people you can work with that you meet in your network, the better the effect for both parties to grow their audiences that way. In my experience it is usually those that you either feel the initiative to take the extra step and continue to communicate beyond social media, or those that do so for you, that end up being the genuine collaborators. Those that shy away from actual phone or face-to-face contact are not usually the ones that end up being collaborated with, though there are exceptions as each may have a specific process or channels when collaborating. This is not to be confused with those whom are willing to communicate at that level but have nothing of real substance or value to offer, as that is just a waste of your time or energy and for simplicity's sake could be considered a form of spam or scam that should be avoided like the plague. Thus speaking from the context of an already qualified potential collaborator, you need to be sure that you can each offer something to each other. For example performing an interview, guest-blogging or promoting a current campaign, if you do that for the other, the other should do the equivalent for you. If the person is much higher profile than you, that in itself becomes the incentive to you. It is also courteous to return the favour when one initiates to do it for you. This can form strong bonds for even deeper connections and teamwork, which always has more of an impact with less struggle than trying to grow your account completely with your own efforts. Still you can remain independent and flexible mutually, not always having to be concerned with cash or recruiting processes, since it should stem from mutual interest, ending up potentially reflecting itself as bartering. Either way, you can negotiate a fair trade.

Also it is not usually the kind of person you meet and suddenly collaborate with unless you are both on parallel paths in your interests and can therefore have a lot to relate to immediately upon first contact. In fact this is a pattern I have noticed, those that you feel as if you have almost known them before the first time you meet, or as if you "get each other" are the ones you are most likely to successfully collaborate with. This is also more interesting for your audience in a sense, since it creates more dynamic content that is not always centralizing a lone figure or aloof brand, but instead an involved person and savvy company, doing things which are more interesting than just the plain old average. It is a way to learn from each other too as well as exchange ideas for mutual growth.

Probably the most challenging part of collaborating is consistency, but I have seen time and time again those that can manage it always have excellent results, assuming everything else is up to par as well. Though being consistent in your own discipline and individual efforts can be a challenge in and of itself, doing so with another is even trickier at times since it requires more conditions be met, such as aligning times and organizing enough to be able to pull it off effectively. With a lot of practice doing content production on your own in advance or live, you will have an easier time doing so with others. The power of doing this is undeniable and is a great way for both parties involved to show a different side of their personalities or ethics due to the nature of you influencing each other and bringing out in each other new angles of who you really are. This helps the audience to see you in a fresh light.

Multiple Accounts

Now that you have learned how to expand the network reach by growing followers on one account, besides having to actually apply the above and get good at it, you can also begin leveraging this newly acquired strength by applying it to multiple accounts if you wish. All you need is a unique email for each account you want to open up. Though I have seen others do this by creating multiple Twitter accounts under the same name and avatar, I seriously would recommend against that. I even polled my audience at one point to see what they thought, and as I thought, they thought that such a 'strategy' is quite a strange thing to do. I would have to agree, however for completely different brands, it is a no-brainer. I have an account for each of multiple brands besides one for my own personal brand. I have one for Production Hackers as well as several others, but the point is that each of them is distinct. Though there may be some overlaps between their niches, so you can expand the reach of one by starting with the following of the other, they still will have to go on each of their own paths in that regard, especially when the niches are quite distinct from each other. When there is overlap however, you can also use one to promote the other.

It is not as cut and dry as you may think though as you usually need the stronger account to promote the weaker ones to have a positive effect, the reverse does not tend to be as effective, but especially if you can provide engaging content on your stronger account that mentions the tag of the other profile, it does actually work to increase the followers of the other brand without having to follow new people. This is really starting to think outside of the box but as you might imagine, especially if you want to run proper content strategies on each account, it can be time-consuming however there is a potential benefit in the long run. Especially if you ensure that the brands you create have each a very focused niche and that the way you present and market it is not tied to your other accounts. Growing a large enough following on it, especially if you are creating engagement (something covered more in depth later) you can sell it as a valuable account to another business in that niche who does not have their social media game on point and wants an immediate solution. You can no longer use the site Twalue.com to estimate a price, before it shut down it was the main tool to value an account, usually valuing each mutual follower at $0.50 while each fan (that you do not follow back) at $1.00. This would have made sense a few years ago, but I would say that mutual followers may now be algorithmically more valuable than they were then. So you could estimate about $0.75 per follow for a rough estimate of what you could price your account to sell to another person. The actual sales process will require you to understand how to sell of course, something also covered later on in this book, but in these kinds of sales it has less to do with tactics, and more to do with patience, like selling a large item on eBay would, since a 10,000+ followed account could potentially sell for $7,500 or more.

Whether you realize it or not, these accounts that you build are like digital real-estate. You investing your time and effort to grow an account is equivalent to building a digital structure that you can sell off to another landlord for him or her to run their own operation, similar to selling a small business to a new owner, if at a micro level and for online communications and lead generation. Growing accounts and selling them can be a lucrative business in itself, especially if you are not going at it all alone and are smart with the niches you pick to grow accounts around. Growing an account quickly with a lot of momentum is extremely challenging to do when you follow less people back, though it is still very possible. Assuming that you are not at that advanced level then I would suggest that if you are planning to grow an account in order to sell it that it has at least around 12-15,000 followers before you decide to sell it. The reason is, even if you follow the advice inside this book, when you unfollow all of those that are following you to increase its monetary value, you can expect a good 15-25% to unfollow you while an account that has less than 10,000 genuine targeted followers may not be worth the effort in selling. Furthermore if you do not follow most of what is taught in this book plus you unfollow everyone, I have heard of people losing a total of 50% of their following by doing that so it can be a really risky thing to do, since if you do successfully sell such an account, the rapid loss of followers to the new owner could end up being quite negative for your reputation which could hurt your future business as well. Therefore continuing to follow back most followers is better for engagement and to keep growing more easily even if it appears less "Celebrity" so you can decide which style you prefer for your situation.

Besides using multiple accounts to promote each other or to build and sell to relevant clients, getting your feet wet in all of the above without risking the embarrassment of a company or brand can be achieved by practicing with other brand accounts you create that you are less concerned with the success of as a training grounds to practice how to do it for the accounts you do care more about. Moreover it is also a way to experiment with content when developing content strategies when you have other accounts with unique brands in the same niche to find what may work before implementing such content into your main account. It is also a way to drive momentum to a particular Tweet you make without having to rely on anyone else, by simply using your alternate accounts with overlapping niches to engage those Tweets yourself making those posts also more appealing for onlookers not wanting to be the first one to engage. This strategy only has a certain degree of effectiveness however, as figuring out what people will actually engage with, without you artificially boosting it, is actually much more valuable to know, but sometimes you need all the advantages you can get, especially when it is something you really want a lot of exposure for, has only a tiny likelihood of getting high engagement yet is something you genuinely consider important to get out there regardless. After you get past those training wheels you will learn more engaging approaches to communicating the same messages. Ideally as mentioned earlier in the book, you would verify unusually high engagement in the post before sharing it one by one through messages or any other channel.

You can really get creative when managing multiple accounts as you can probably gather by what I have already explained in this section and I am sure you can come up with multiple strategies yourself when doing this, but perhaps the greatest value may be if you are hoping to run a social media marketing agency service, buying and selling accounts or marketing yourself or your business. By practising the management of growing multiple accounts successfully, you will have what it takes to take on multiple clients' accounts and grow them all simultaneously while you grow your own. Also if you grow enough accounts strongly enough, you can always use them as social proof when you start out with such an agency service since your new prospects and potential clients will usually want to see where you have successfully grown other accounts besides the one where they found you. Ideally you can refer them to other clients profiles you have worked on but when just starting out this can turn into a catch-22 situation where you need proof of growing other accounts before you can get a client to trust you to grow your first account other than your own. Of course some clients, even when expressing supposedly genuine interest may never be convinced enough no matter what you show them, but those are probably not the ones you want to deal with as there are many fish in the sea, but we will save expanding on that point in the chapter on sales.

A quick tip for the moment is to run a free trial of your service, if you can afford it. This is to gain trust in your ability to provide results, and be able to offer a paid service from there.

As you probably realize by this point, the possibilities are really endless even when it comes to growing accounts alone, and we have not even covered the marketing or sales part yet! You may have not realized how deep this can really go, maybe even thinking that social media was a trend or passing fad, but perhaps at this point you are learning it could be turned into a university program with a certification or diploma receivable at the end. Any business can be run, besides the meta examples in this chapter. You can think more micro like promoting a personal project you are working on or something you are involved with in a team. Using multiple accounts is an excellent way to try split-testing within the same market, just as well as it being a powerful tool for testing multiple markets and taking out-of-the-box approaches inside the box of Twitter.

Engaging Followers

Content Strategy

The fact that I am teaching for the solo individual who can become a complete social media influencer bootstrapping, without a team is effectively achieving what most real entrepreneurs would deem a pipe dream. Actually achieving tangible and big results as an expert of social media growth is a testament to my having learned the skills through trial and error. That is besides the notion that these same strategies could indeed be scaled out into a team for multiplied effect though, as I have stated, unnecessary to have substantial status if you know the right way as taught in this book, are disciplined and get good at it, but there is more to this book than just growing an enviable following with some simple tips and strategies to put into action for about 30-60 minutes a day as already taught herein. What I am referring is to content strategy and if you were going to learn one thing from this entire book, that would be it. It is of higher value than the entire last chapter, not to undermine the highly sought out value therein, and also more at the core of what is most important beyond sales or prospecting, even beyond social media its very self, but I will stay appropriately within the context of this book's focus of social media in order to explain it.

The content strategy as referred to, is truly the most elusive science that I can teach in this text and the principles involved underneath the surface are transferrable to pretty much anything you could ever want to achieve in life, business, sales, investment or the subject being covered in this chapter; marketing. That is because it has to be customized to your conditions. It is the essence of successful marketing at its core and something which can never be emphasized, reiterated or covered enough.

This is the ultimate advanced Twitter guide and I hope this section makes it worth the price. The truth is I cannot measure the level of value of this information, so whatever it took you to get you here, to take the leap of faith, to trust me as your guide and to then actually invest the time and energy required to learn this stuff and get here; I have absolute confidence it was completely worth it. Although I can say that often when promoting this book, in attempts to persuade you through marketing campaigns, social proof and absolute conviction with every possible touch point, every single angle I can reach you from every level; it will never change the fact that you have to take the teaching to heart for it to actually work so that is why I have not been concerned about being overly secretive with this information nor am I worried that I will not be able to represent the value of it. I know it is something that could be taught or studied forever regardless, so I will make sure to bring you what is most pertinent and important to consider within this context instead of trying to explain my life away.

That is not to say that if you do not get what I am talking about here there is no hope for what is so special, what makes this so revolutionary since this is not some complex form of thinking and sophistication that you can never understand nor am I suggesting that you should quit now; it is to say that this stuff is very easy to overlook, take for granted miss the point and simply seem esoteric which is why I am framing it this way in hopes that you can wake up and see the true worth of what I am disseminating here. It might sound like I am all of a sudden bringing you to church, taking you to the temple of illumination, evangelizing a spiritual world or referring to religious undertakings, but there is a good reason for that; that is what is required to express the level of integrity to the teaching found in the real meat and potatoes, the real substance of what everyone of competence should understand. Not only cerebrally, theoretically or via the memorization of some static knowledge, but at the instinctual level where it is not separate from you nor from your very core, not something to employ or a magic trick to pull off, but really one with your very being and who you truly are.

With that out of the way we can get right into what the first point I would like to make about marketing yourself on Twitter is, truly achieving the mysterious feat of genuine engagement without having to cheat, use cheap tricks or implement guerrilla tactics to enjoy its fruits. As you may have guessed, doing all of the above could make it seem like you are accomplishing the desired results, but when you look back at the data, the actual numbers and analytics, the actuality cannot be altered; the numbers do not lie, and this is absolutely no exception. Though you might see someone on social media with posts getting dozens, hundreds, thousands or more likes, shares, or comments, it is not always clear how that was achieved as those that make use of artificial methods of achieving that are mixed in with those that actually have hit upon the gold rush of "virality." In fact there are cases where one influencer or guru may have what appears to be much less engagement than another where the truth is behind the scenes, that brand is getting more. This can be knowingly or even with that social media influencer not even realizing that is the case, him or herself. How can this be? As I said it all comes down to science, math, numbers based on human psychology and more. You may be thinking there is no way anything about a marketing book teaching social media could have that amount of importance outside of some mere tools and strategies to expand the business in more and better ways. Just like the many other resources and teachings out there I fully admit that and will not pretend that the underlying principles are not contained from other sources, just that its application, especially at the level of mastery, within the context of social media is rare at best. I would even go as far to say that this is truly the key behind the success of not only the most impactful online influencers, but of those in any kind of business whatsoever, even if it is under a different set of rules, terminology, conditions or makeup. That is because this is just as much what makes the difference between a successful political campaign or a failure; this is at the essence of science and humanity all in one. It simply comes down to paying attention to what the world is telling you and responding within your integrity again and again to the point where that turn-based relationship can develop to a point of harmony where you are providing what is hoped for in a way that is in line with what you truly enjoy. This happens to parallel the concept of 'Ikigai' covered by several other authors, and may be worth the added research. "VENN" diagrams demonstrating it may make it even easier for you to grasp visually.

Sharing Content

"SO WHAT IS IT!?" is what you may be asking, with my talking like a preacher, prophet or motivational speaker, you may be feeling, out of nowhere. I keep saying things like "content strategy" as well as "science," "psychology," and "core" with you may be feeling that I am never actually getting to the point but as I have stated again and again, I will do my best to make this comprehensible and digestible for you considering what this book is supposed to help you with specifically and cover; making a legitimate business out of your social media presence, particularly Twitter.

Keeping it simple, as increased sophistication and complexity may help generate interest and be marketable to the impressionable facets of human sensitivities and perceptions, it is rather the simplest, most fundamental, essentially minimal and laser-focused way that will cut through and production hack your results (see what I did there?). Thus whether or not you are convinced or not at the importance and golden ticket that this information really is or not, it does not really matter, as like I wrote earlier, you will only be able to understand what I am disseminating as far as your current comprehension has already been reached, so to really reach a new level from studying this you need to be willing to be open to the outer limits and edges of everything you have ever thought, known, imagined, believed or experienced; yes it is that kind of thing, so let us get into it shall we?

As this section is referred to as experimentation, I do not just want to teach it, I want to exemplify it and that is why you may have noticed the very feeling and style of this chapter's introductory paragraphs seem at least a little different than the rest and that is due to the fact that even the very way I am writing these very words for you is at its root a kind of experiment (and a run on sentence!), because as it is said "it is one thing to tell you what you should do, but it is a whole other thing to show you what to do" thus my very intention here is to actuate both simultaneously as you read it. These longer sentences - though often frowned upon - work like streams of consciousness that perform as they inform, with some of the greatest quotes in history, such as those by President Abraham Lincoln, being very notable examples.

Without trying to get too pretentious, pedantic nor get too involved in creating new words and breaking standard conventions of communications, let us stick to what you can begin experimenting with today. Let us take your journey from one of expansion and breadth, the main focus in the last chapter on growth, towards one of narrowing down your niche and going deeper. Though some of you reading this may feel, especially the younger and hipper of you, that when I am talking about going in depth, it is something that has so far been more difficult to you, depending also on your personality type regardless of age or crowd you identify yourself with, while others within you may be thinking you already know what depth is and it is as simple as committing to focusing on a certain discipline, field or "going with what you know" but that is just scratching the surface, as it is only the context of what I am talking about, not the content. From what I have observed, beyond merely how things appear to be, but really understanding what goes on behind the scenes to uncover the real truth of the matter, I am confident that if any of you truly knows completely what I am talking about here you are most likely a rarity within a rarity, no matter how simple the information herein might seem. This is because this is something I have only witnessed a fraction within a fraction of people ascertain consistently, and it is so vital to differentiating your brand that I can be certain that even among those figures, attention will be had to what is learnable here since it is a subject that requires that level of immersion after all and will be weaved into every other part of everything you do from the growth aspect, to the sales, to the various sections on scaling it up found in this book.

"Ideas. Make. Ideas. Make. Ideas! Make!"
\- Gary Vaynerchuk

Like a lot of other books I could have tortured you by saving this section for last and you may be thinking that after this chapter it will be hard to live up to it, but there is a method to my madness. Why I am covering it here rather than later, avoiding the "put them through the dry and heavy first before getting to the good stuff?" That is a method that many authors rely upon in order to have the contents of their texts work like a reward system in that only those that stuck it through until the end deserve to get to the best part. However if you know me at any level and have even come as far as this second chapter, you may already know I am not only different than the crowd but can even be different than the leaders without compromising what makes up a leader nor falling in the doughy middle, but rather being completely one-of-kind in my approach even if I do, just as all top performers and influencers, learn from and implement what can be learned from all the best out there. The thing about me as well, is that I am just as much never afraid to figure it out completely for myself and even reinventing the wheel if I have to, though seemingly counter-intuitive, it is not the proverbial wheel itself here that is important but rather the ability create it in the first place, which is why it can be incredibly integral to know how to reinvent it. Imagine if all knowledge, reference points and specialists in wheel creation one day disappeared, being able to start from scratch and solve that problem anew goes from irrelevant to the most important possible thing. Besides, if you really do reinvent the wheel it will never be the exact same wheel anyway and something will differentiate it when it is coming from that pure place. That is why this is so essential, it is not the techniques, strategies tools or steps in themselves that are the most value when it comes to achieving the elusive engagement but rather the mindset that goes behind it all. The purpose of my bringing it up here over doing so later is not just an experiment for the sake of an experiment however but partly because this is the order in which I figured it out, before what is taught in later chapters as well as the fact that I use this aspect as a way to aid what is taught later, so it makes more sense, at least in the way I have discovered it throughout the embarkment of my journey thus far that you understand this first before connecting it to the ever important parts that come.

The craziest part about all this is that, at least from the level of pure social media engagement mastery, this might not necessarily affect your bottom line by itself, but it will help you establish a larger platform for you to create, multiply or increase it. The truth is that the shortcut would be to piggyback on what others are already doing that engages, but what I am covering is innovation instead, which is longer and harder but ultimately more creative, cherished and valuable longterm. Though marketing can increase the size of your cup, it cannot fill it! You need focus in a real business behind the scenes and the follow-through into sales to fill your allegorical cup, then together it is a powerful combination that can increase your overall cash flow and net worth.

That is why really understanding what I am talking about here is beyond any work or practice you can do externally and much more something you have to do internally, within your own mind to genuinely be able to not only do it by fluke but reach that incredibly minute amount of people's level in achieving it. Look at those with the biggest "cups" they're the innovators and one's thinking outside of the box; they stand out like a sore thumb. This is important and the real deal, even if at the level of getting some authentic likes and shares or commentary without phoney trickery or what could be considered unfair tactics, because if you can master it at this level, it can be applied to anything including what is to come which actually does effect the bottom line, the increase of income through sales, if that is your goal, or perhaps it is a social mission or a crusade to change the very way we live as a human race; getting it right at this micro-level, whether you know it or not, will be applicable to anything and everything you could ever want to realize from here on out.

This is as simple as just trying something you never have before, and that is the seed of it - courage - seeing what feedback you get - listening - and then acting accordingly.

The first part; trying something completely new is what experimenting is all about and is the first step in achieving a proper content strategy, so you really need to take a step back and "see the forest for the trees" in order to begin running this so you cannot be afraid to think out of the box, even challenging everything you thought was real; the absolute truth of the process, how things are or how they should be done. You need to be able to literally try anything and everything albeit revolving around who you really are, your values and what your personal brand or company culture is representing (see: 'Ikigai'). That is because of course you want to remain consistent with who you are and what you are trying to do and much of what the first chapter was about making clear. However to take it to the next level you have to break out of your shell and be willing to be courageous enough to try something you never have before, going further even, pushing the edge of your competency limits. You need to be your true self, you have never seen anyone else be you, no matter how well-versed you may be in what is out there even if equivalent; it is your intuitive originality that makes you unique. This is at once extremely simple yet a massive challenge over time but is pivotal to your achieving initial success and eventually massive success.

Therefore do not be afraid to try something different, but do not just do it for the sake of being different. Make sure that it is all coming back to what you are trying to achieve, the principles you stand by and where you want to go, that you do pay attention to what others are doing with success and where others fall short - though innovating inside of that to do something not quite like anyone else - to produce something that may be made up of the same ingredients as anyone or anything else but that is put together in a way that is historical in nature. So whether it is some simple lines of text in a Tweet, a photo you took, content you curated, a meme you found or one you came up with yourself, a video, a poll, a live stream, the *"gämification"* of some aspect of the technology, an innovative use of simple tools, a culture-oriented approach or even a campaign for enlightening the community you have built on a whole new perspective, you have to keep going with the output of the brand new without neglecting what the feedback is so that you can keep on top of what it all means, so that it is not just a random effort for the sake of busy work but an insightful never-ending learning process that forms the foundation to build upon and grow the passion, interest and quality of attention being given to you and what you do by having that creative spark. The interesting part is that many different influencers following this process can develop completely different styles, leaning on one's own unique strength, yet achieve equivalently positive results nonetheless. Doing so all the while remaining attentive, smartly being in tune with what is working and what is not while never being afraid to start from scratch again is all part of it. Even when it seems you finally "got it" and are tempted to just spin your wheels, be complacent and rest on your laurels, you will still need these three elements:

1. Ditching what does not work

2. Doubling down on what does work

3. Doing something completely different to see if it will work or not

As I said, it is as simple as that, as basic as 1-2-3, but in the rest of this chapter I will go more in-depth on what this actually entails on Twitter and the multiple strategies that exemplify it with the various tools available to you, so that you can practice and master how this works on Twitter and potentially more vitally, how you can take these core concepts of why this is central and transfer it to any other medium or objective of your choice. This will allow you to come up with an entire rotation of content that you keep engaging audiences with cyclically, while updating it to remove stale pieces and increase the fresh ones that still engage, eventually gaining a sense of what your particular audience likes without ever losing the essence of what keeps it all fresh.

So give it a try, next time you are on Twitter or your favourite social media site or app of choice, post something different. It does not need to be representing anyone but yourself, but that does not mean you should not step out of your comfort zone, showing more sides to who you are, through more media formats, conventions and creative approaches to really spark the imagination of your network.

Assessing Feedback

Now that you have taken that leap of faith and learned to experiment and try something new continuously, you have got the overall bird's eye view of what it means to implement a working and effective content strategy that is inherently scientific, we can get into the substance of how you can extract value of what you find and how you can actually do this with precision, as it is a kind of science after all. This is all done by assessing the feedback and that is how you build your strategy.

In practice when you put something new out there, whether it be a piece of content, an ad, a pitch or the release of a product or launch of a service, you always need to pay attention to the feedback you are getting. When it comes to content it could be likes or shares, even comments, when it comes to ads, it is also engagement but can include click-throughs after the initial clicks as well as conversions or where their attention is going by using what is called a website heat-map for instance. When it comes to Twitter specifically you have many powerful 3rd-party tools, but the one tool that I use the most is not 3rd-party but built right into Twitter these days, and is based on the technology from the stand-alone site, Twitter Analytics, which I have already made you familiar with up to this point. It is through the Twitter Analytics systems that you can get all the data that can allow you to know what your feedback actually is beyond just what you see on the surface, the amount of likes, shares and comments but just as well the clicks, the media views and so on as well. We already went over figuring out the engagement percentage using these tools but let us go a little deeper shall we?

You can start to get more creative with strategies to not only double down on what is getting the most response and cutting out what is being left cold by your audience but taking it a step further and reaching out to those people, not only to sell to them necessarily, as that is covered later but to find out more what the person likes. This would be reflected practically as seeing that list of people who liked, commented and shared the content in your notifications and opening up a DM conversation with those individuals. Although that is also the same kind of strategy used to prospect and get them to close on a deal or get closer to them through preferred contact so that one can invest or commit to you… at this stage it is actually a combination of building the groundwork. It is important simultaneously to be deepening your understanding, with pinpoint precision of your potential customers' or clients' real wants and needs. Beyond this you might not want to sell anything at all, perhaps you are recruiting people to work for you or you are seeking out mentorship; in truth any kind of relationship is possible. Of course polling your audience regularly also achieves this, but there is a caveat to relying on poll data itself. The fact of the matter is that even though your polls might reflect that one point is way more appealing and popular than another in the choices, you should never neglect the votes that came in for the other choices as well even if smaller in number, because you can use all of that information rather than the poll winners alone to develop your strategy.

The fact of the matter is that the poll winners, at least from within the context of your audience will always have more mainstream appeal so it is an excellent way to attract more of your people by giving them what they want. By providing them exactly what most of them chose over the other options, it is an excellent way to increase *virality* time and again except for rare cases I have found this to multiply the engagement you get, especially compared to an averagely engaging post. Of course if it is a current trending topic as well, that may help too, but your angle on it may only work if you are genuinely interested. However the problem is that although poll winners can have mass appeal that does not mean that the passion is necessarily as high as those more unique and different individuals who do not think the same as the pack and did not choose a popular choice, so should not be neglected. In fact it is more likely that the people who chose the less mainstream option are the ones with greater passion for those things. Especially because if it really is going against the grain, it is less likely easy for them to find, giving them even more incentive to get it from whomever can provide it. To put it simply, your poll winners should be used as a marketing tool to increase your overall engagement, get more attention and ultimately attract more people, yet the ones that did receive votes (assuming not 0) that you can integrally provide for may actually be more loyal, willing to pay more and be more appreciative of your provisions even if not the winning choice(s) of the poll.

One important technical note regarding engagement on polls should be pointed out as well. Since about early 2018 or so Twitter Analytics has changed the way it reports engagement on polls. If you look at the list of engaged metrics in a poll's analytics, you will notice the vote count does not match with the vote count of the poll itself. There has been a new policy to cut a huge portion of the votes from the engagement score and is no longer accurate. Thankfully the simple way to solve this is to use the actual poll's vote number displayed in the Tweet in place of the cut one listed in analytics to add your score with your detailed metrics on that Tweet, to be able to calculate the right percentage.

There is another problem in that maybe the voters are not as aware of themselves as you might think, confusing the meaning of the poll choices for instance. That goes along with many unknown factors that could contribute to inaccuracy or even the possibility that things are literally what they seem, even to the point that those who did not vote the poll winner could change their minds after seeing what took the crown. Therefore it is hard to tell exactly what everything means, though it is of course providing you insight to lead you into the right direction, you are going to need a way to more specifically find out. That will be subject matter you will then bring out when you are reaching out one-on-one through DMs to engaged followers. First of all doing so with a proper human greeting when you make first contact and waiting for a response rather than attempting to hawk your product. Instead ask for insight into the person with questions about their greatest challenges, needs, or greatest preferences so you can learn what kind of person is behind which response so you can then use that as arms for deciding what the poll results actually mean.

For instance if you asked "What's your fave hot sauce?" and tobasco won. Let us say there was still a group of people that voted sriracha, instead of absolutely assuming that you should double down on tobasco and only sell that with that as the end of your research, rather going and DMing those that engaged with the poll using likes or shares, or even those that have engaged with your other content regardless of the poll, asking *those people* what problem you can solve for them, their likes and dislikes so that you can start to get a better idea of whom is who when it comes to voters behind the poll.

You may find that although most people in your audience like tobasco, those that actually engage in your content, which are actually more likely to trust you may in fact prefer sriracha, so that is why it is valuable to DM them to take your relationship to the next level and appeal to them, the true engagers first instead of just following the crowd on the data. To bring in even more relevancy you can feature tobasco as a main attraction, putting sriracha as a premium alternative for instance. This way you can increase the mass appeal of what you are doing by doubling down on what wins yet you can simultaneously take action to appeal to the genuine niches therein as well. Thus the best way to be sure is that one-on-one communication that lets you know what not only the average person is thinking in your audience but going as far as finding out what the extraordinarily faithful in you think and believe to appease to the quality in your audience over the quantity. Meaning as you attract many by following the winners of the poll, you can have more progress quicker and better by executing on what you found out about the small choices that got some votes instead, the people behind them that are likely to buy from you more than those just passing by and enjoying your poll, now you can actually DM them in an appreciative and conversational manner to build your rapport while learning the deeper truths of your audience. At the same time you are priming those relationships to be those that take the first bite out of your monetizing what you provide, thus fairly giving those people the most benefit. You may find that more general everyday topics will engage more for the most part than specific niche topics, yet it is the results from the niche polls that are going to provide you more business value. The general topics, like Twitter's template "What's happening?" are instead better for increasing the reach of your brand rather than conversions. That is also very valuable however, the same reason major brands use celebrity endorsements to increase their reach, it may not lead to immediate sales, but it may increase the potential relationships of all kinds, the "sale" is in the follow-up. I would recommend going by the principles of "Jab, Jab, Jab, Right Hook" by Gary Vaynerchuk, for a great idea of how this works; in the end the unconditional giver (that can afford to be so) will be the one that attracts the most quality relationships, regardless of if it is for business or personal.

Tweet Limit

"Do what you did yesterday & tomorrow is the same!"
\- Anik Singal

I wanted to add that while writing this book I came upon something new I never knew existed, I learned that not only are there the imposed limits we spoke about in the last section, there is also a limit to how many times you can Tweet a day. It is quite high however though split up by the hour. That number is about 100 Tweets/Hour but I have found it is not so cut and dry, meaning I have been able to Tweet more than 100 times in an hour, as long as I did not just Tweet 100 times in the previous hour, but specifically once you try to Tweet 2 hours + worth of content according to the limits (about 2-300 Tweets) it will give you that limit reach where you can no longer Tweet again unless you wait about an hour or two. This is usually not a problem and in fact, even if all that content you are Tweeting has been engaging more than 1.0% as we spoke about earlier, maybe at that point it is time to step up your game and make your engagement percentage higher at that point to reduce the amount of content you may rotate. You can also, instead of tweet storming, a strategy I use, be a bit more organized and run those Tweets through a scheduler, as there are many solutions like that available. As recommended, if you have built up such a large amount of engaging content that you are hitting the Tweet Limit, then up your standard for the engagement percentage as a practical strategy that forces you to get on a whole new level of engagement. It also should be noted there are 'like' limits as well if you really go nuts with that heart icon.

Campaigning Actions

Most people assume when they want to run a campaign, they just need to launch and promote it, but then again most people fail in their campaign goals, so taking the approach that most people decide to take is clearly not a wise choice. Instead those that have actually done the research, watched those that succeeded, doggedly learned from trial and error or a combination of the above will tell you that you need to run a pre-campaign before the launch of your actual campaign. This is similar to the phenomena of providing a lot of free content that is a testing grounds for seeing what gets the most positive feedback before launching products based on those results, though of course even the products themselves are a research tool, when you can assess which were the most popular. Campaigns are no different in that you actually need to develop the strategy for gaining people's attention and engagement before your campaign officially launches. You can take the information and data gained from that pre-campaign and implement what you learned in the campaign itself. Building up the momentum to the launch of the campaign in advance with a pre-campaign that allows everyone to be ready and primed for when the official campaign starts where one could buy the product or service, invest as a funder or as a special interest, it always applies the same. By the time you launch you have done a number of things; you have gotten people to know that this is going to happen long before it happens, you have used the content strategy principles to develop the framing of the marketing, focusing on the audience's problem. You are innovative in how you are providing a solution for within the language and culture of those people and once again campaigning from the beginning at launch. This time for the conversions of your income generation or fundraising model once the campaign proper is launched. From there you should get way more people investing from the start until you reach a peak of activity of outcomes from your continuous campaigning. This usually lasts maybe a week or two, depending on whether your campaign will be limited up to a certain time, when the activity of conversions or revenue generation starts to dip, you can then pivot the angle on your campaign, as if launching a third campaign for this one project within the whole singular campaign process, this time building up momentum towards the fact that the chance for people to invest will close soon, so that by the time it does end, there will be a whole new slew of people supporting in order to avoid losing out on the chance. At that point being told through your promotional measures that there is a limit and it is coming up. Then they are most likely, the closer it is to the end of the campaign, to put in their dollars to prevent missing out on the opportunity to be part of the movement with all its tangible and intangible benefits.

During the campaign itself you need to stand out and think differently so attacking from every angle is key. Looking up trending words on Google or Youtube and of course, Twitter itself, wrapping your campaign around the keywords most relevant to you to get more reach and build more hype. You can also look up the latest news in your field and leverage that topic to promote your campaign. Pretty much combine all the aspects of engagement concentrated around this one thing you want to promote.

You can find hot conversations with a lot of people or high profile accounts participating in a subject that is somehow relevant to your offer and join in. From there you can find a way to naturally tie it into your offer over the long run, after those new people warm up to you and your content. This ensures that people do not feel like you are only trying to sell something because you are coming into the conversation naturally as anyone else, yet allowing yourself the chance to sell anyway by organically tying it back into what you are doing when appropriate. Ideally your participation in hot topics can have others ask you what it is you do which is a great way to convince them your sharing is genuine rather than contrived which is key to having the likelihood of them getting to know, like and trust you which is necessary to achieve more of what you want in your business and life. By being who you are while placing yourself in the right situations during the most relevant times, the right opportunities come to you without having to appeal to something you are not, nor having to constantly chase for results. As usual what works is authenticity so if you can manage to continuously work through your insecurities, your true self will shine.

At this point you need all the attention you can get by standing out among the crowd so using the powerful tools readily available to you in an unorthodox way is a great ticket to have people pay some serious attention to what you are doing. There are a few examples where I have potentially innovated on the platform, doing what I had seen none do up to that point such as creating a choose-your-own adventure with a series of polls, doing a battle of the polls, taking the winners of multiple polls and facing them off, or DMing embedded tweets with rich media content, something you can do as well with catchy themes and subject matter in tune with your brand; the reason why people followed you in the first place. Being more creative and generous with content on a platform designed for communications makes it easier to stand out. Same goes for emphasizing communication on content platforms like Instagram or YouTube; complimenting the environment you are in to fill the void and meet the awareness of those actively engaging those spaces often is a recipe for positive results.

Blowing Up A Post

Now that you have been developing your content strategy to the point that you have a bunch of Tweets that you retweet in rotation along with the new ones you try out (while removing the ones that begin to go under your standard for engagement) you can begin the prospecting strategy that is covered more deeply in the next section. The strategy I use is to go and reach out, one-on-one with DMs in a natural conversational manner, as opposed to asking for something right away, to the ones who have engaged with your post, ideally those that have engaged with you more than once, but you are still pretty safe to approach those who have done it for their first time if you stick to speaking with consideration in a natural tone. You can even go in cold if you are coming from a place of contribution rather than taking. After some light chatting, you can then go ahead and inform them of a Tweet you made in particular you want to get more engagement and why it would be good for them to do so, and you will find that if you have gotten this far, with proper responses and communications from when you opened up the DM conversation, most will be happy to retweet the tweet in question. Another way of course is tit for tat, you promising to retweet for a retweet, though I recommend it happen more naturally since then its more likely your mutual audiences will benefit and engage, not only sharing to get shared. Once they do, make sure to give a big thank you and moreover to keep the conversation going, even if suggesting you continue to chat later.

This is an excellent way to make a post get organic, unpaid engagement, without it having to rely on it being engaging based on its merits; before many others have taken the leap. However if you combine this technique with those that are already engaging, you do not even have to frame it so much as them helping you, but rather you bringing up something to them that they would likely be interested in and therefore benefit from participating. That is of course considering you are maintaining that natural tone and not bringing it up until it seems appropriate if rather assertively and as soon as possible regardless. This is a way to take a Tweet that maybe has 1-2% engagement and multiply that by 2-10X the likes and retweets in a relatively quick time without even having to set up any kind of promotional campaign that would cost you your hard earned dollars. Since this can be time-consuming however, I usually save it for particular posts I want a lot of traction, even if they are already engaging. A great example is when I live stream interviews and want to be sure that the interviewee is getting a lot of value by increasing their reach that way. This can also be done before you even post it, prepping people in your audience to engage with it once it is tweeted. This works best for engaging posts, as I have said but you might be wondering "How in cases where it has not been tweeted yet, would you know that it will be engaging enough?" Although you can never know how much a post will actually engage before you post it, from experience honing all of the above in this book so far, you can make an educated guess. For example; a poll, a stream or a meme about relatable, trending or humorous subjects with stark, witty, compelling or catchy delivery, even touching journalism; certain types of content just happen to engage more than others. You can then do that advanced invitation strategy with more confidence.

Increasing Value With Lists

"To follow back or not to follow back, that is the question!"

The advanced strategies you can employ are driving traffic to your account from other accounts or other places whether on other social media, websites or even from people in real life. You can use advertising or even collaborate with other influencers to promote each other's accounts, all more challenging than the simple strategies laid out in the first chapter. You can even do an advanced version of that strategy in the growth section following 800 per day instead of 400, by waiting about 12-16 hours since the last time you mass followed, then ensuring you only unfollow those that did not follow back after 24 hours from the first 400 you followed without unfollowing the 2nd group of 400 you followed 8-12 hours earlier, meaning you will need to keep track of the separate groups of people you followed, which, with some practice, is not as hard as you might think.

One major tip I will put out there that a lot of smaller accounts seem not to follow is to simply unfollow those that are not following you after some time, even though I mentioned this as part of the growth strategy, it also adds value when you are not trying to grow your account to follow less of the people that do not follow you. This also decreases openings for scammers since it leaves less ways for others to message you without actually showing interest in anything but getting something from you. This makes it better for when you are reaching the campaign stage wasting less time and energy on those that are not really following you for what you have to offer, but simply for their own network reach or other selfish interests.

An incredible way to use the power of SocialRank is combined with Twitter's list feature. With some advanced preparation, based on one niche at a time, add all the followers you would like to a list in Twitter, filtered for free by SocialRank (or otherwise). After you have done this for all your desired interests or niches you will have a list of lists to refer to in Twitter, each with their own timeline style feeds featuring only those curated by each interest in realtime. This increases the practicality of your account quite a bit making it much more monetarily valuable. This is also important for fans that you do not follow back as it is one of the only ways to see what they are posting by making a list of them as a group without potentially hitting an unnecessary following limit. If you are not searching based on certain criteria and want to find who is following you but whom you are not, the most basic ability to simply look at your followers' activity becomes a higher value feature, so lists fill that gap. You can even make lists of those that do not follow you at all - whether with your main account or an alternate - whether for entertainment or research purposes; either way.

Some advantages of following less superfluously is less noise in your home feed. You can also apply different strategies such as following only the highest value prospects you have qualified to greatly deepen your relationship. The rule taught by some of the top businesspeople in the world is that you only need "1000 true fans" to have a successful business. Through all the different strategies and methods of qualification you can, they will all make it easier to curate a real community whether it be for personal or business purposes.

Building Relationships

Responding Directly

With a highly targeted following based on niche and location built up by implementing what was learned in the previous chapters, you could simply go into your following and start DM conversations, ideally organically. Not automated, neither without a human touch in your approach, you can use the fact that they are following you as a lead in to break the ice. This can be further aided, as you should know by this point, with your content strategy, so you can already know that the person is not just following you, but also was somehow moved enough to engage with at least one of your posts, meaning that person is also likely to engage again in the future which is great for social proof of your account's legitimacy and for knowing who to approach first. Though you might get a reasonable number of people engaging, if they have already been qualified as people for you to get to follow you in the first place, and now even further with their showing engagement, you should take it a step further. Take a quick look at their bio to have some confidence that they could be a real valuable contact for you in the future. From there you can open up a conversation with a greeting of your own or use the one shared with you in the next section as a basic example to get your feet wet, which you can use as a template to build your own, as well as some pointers to keep it authentic.

Though a portion of these leads will have a website provided on their profile which will in turn have a phone number you can call, doing the above first allows you to give them some awareness before receiving any calls from you, making you someone other than just a cold caller. You can even call if they did not yet respond to your messages because you have a lot of leeway when you combine the fact the person has followed, has heard of you, has engaged with you, thus probably like you, and you have approached him or her in a conversational, natural and human way. This allows them to better trust you. No two potential clients, partners or mentors are the same, so play with your methods of communication to find the best approach for each person, especially when it is a more longterm prospect. Therefore when you are calling that person you can have massive confidence in yourself knowing that you already have that connection, a greater mindshare and recognition with him or her. In the next section I will also go over how you can schedule a call through the DMs for even warmer calls.

Though a lot of it is meant to be a way to have offsite contact in order to close the gap between you and the prospect, there are highly recommended ways to do so right within Twitter's DMs natively if you recognize the person is highly responsive there already. The best examples of this - a technique which can also be used when Tweeting at people with their full handle - is to record a short personal video for that person only. When it is DMed to that person instead of Tweeted however, where no one else can see it, Twitter's lack of a built-in private live video chat feature is overcome, pushing the tech to its edge, providing 100% customized rich media, which has you stand out; really making the most of Twitter's smaller cup in terms of functionality versus other social media. It also provides you a good excuse to keep them there if they want you to switch to a communication channel you may not prefer.

Building Conversations

Now that you have built your following, and content strategy and have found the engagers, who you have then reviewed their profile to qualify them as quality leads, you can start that conversation, but you may be wondering "What should I say?" and "How should I say it?" Well you bought this book, so I want to make sure that you get your money's worth so I will provide with a template for greeting right here which, even without a response is a primer for your first call nonetheless out of the ones that have a phone number available on their website, and even if they do not, you can still go ahead and send a follow-up message the next time that account engages, which has fair likelihood considering they already have engaged in the past. What will be provided for you is something different, a template for the kind of messages you could send. However before that, I want to mention some quick pointers to help you. You can click on a message you sent and get the option to have Twitter delete it for you, this also works if you tap it on a mobile device. Another point is when referring to the individual or company make sure not only to look at the name they are calling themselves at the top of their profile but also the tag as well, since sometimes the actual name is not in the title but in the tag and vice versa, otherwise you can leave the name out or even use it as a funny talking point asking something like "is that the name you go by?" or "is it Ok if I call you that?" or even "what name do you prefer to go by?" which are excellent conversation starters in themselves and something a robot, at least at this point, would probably not do! Finally I wanted to mention to *not* send the entire greeting in one message block. You want every line or phrase to be its own message, as that is how one would naturally converse, otherwise, though it may seem easier to do so, it will look like you are copy and pasting the message to everyone which, if that was the case, you might as well be using an auto-responder which we have already determined is incredibly ineffective. Of course if it is an embedded tweet (by simply posting the link to the tweet as is as a message) it looks better than a long DM block especially if it offers rich media content, but in either case you want to avoid appearing like an auto-responder. I even did a poll on auto-responders and the vast majority despised them!

Greeting Template

Message 1: Hello [Insert Name Here] <- Title OR Tag

Message 2: it's a pleasure to connect with you

Message 3: I hope you're doing well

Message 4: just wanted to thank you for your ongoing support

Message 5: It is much appreciated

At this point in the greeting, you wait for a response and move onto the next person in the meantime, using the exact same process already discussed for vetting them.

Greeting Response

Prospect M1: Thank you!

Message 6: You're welcome, anytime.

Message 7: Never hesitate to let me know if I can ever be of help or service to you.

Prospect M2: Great, likewise, I'll keep that in mind.

Message 8: Fantastic, learn more by scheduling a call

Alternate message 8: Fantastic, you can learn more by signing up for my newsletter at this link: [place link here]

***

Of course you can modify the above to fit your needs and style, shorten it or change the phrases, you may not even need to do a direct call to action right there, but post a tweet link that will be embedded with its own call to action in the text or media. It was once ideal to get them on a call, whether on the phone or video teleconferencing, as that tends to be most effective for closing deals, but it is not always necessary based on the person you are dealing with, however just in case be prepared to require a full video call. It is that simple yet if everybody knew and did that so many would not be complaining that social media is "ineffective" for getting quality leads and prospecting.

Closing The Deal

Now with all of the above, such as shown in my sugary sweet example of what a conversation might look like up to scheduling a call (as you may know it is not always going to be that easy), that does not mean; even if you have many fish in your established sea, that you should simply move on as there are some things you can do even if the person responds that they will "do it later" or "not right now" or any such objection. This can be done by asking 3 questions which will be the final qualifier which you can do after objections to the above in the DMs or even if you call them on the phone after making that initial contact, whether the person or representative responded or not. These questions are great not only for leading the party into what you have to offer, but ensuring one is actually worth your time and business. Asking these questions in a DM would happen if the person has responded to your initial greeting and is showing some interest but is not biting right away on the scheduled call, to sign up to your newsletter form, for instance, which ideally includes a slot for their phone numbers on top of the emails as well or any other way of getting their direct contact information or action. If the questions do get responded to in a DM, from there there is more incentive to schedule a more in-depth call and for you to offer to send them a detailed email about your offerings, potentially doing both to make it the most convenient for them. However depending on the person, there are cases where everything can be handled in the DM, but of course being able to text their phone is even better which as you should know requires your trust. Otherwise if the person has not responded to your DMs at all, not only do you have a lot of leverage with all your contact based on qualification and shown interest from him or her so far, when you actually get them on that initial (non-scheduled) call or you find their email, you can use these questions to know whether this can lead to a real deal, sale or commitment otherwise you can stop there and move onto the next prospect.

Three Questions

1. *How do you like your current [equivalent product or service]?*

2. *Will you do any changes to it within the next 3-6 months?*

3. *When can we schedule a call? (If they are local you can say "When can we schedule a meeting?" instead)*

When you ask the above it really gives you, after the person responds, the knowledge you need to take it a step further and follow up with that detailed call or email where you want to present your entire offer and how it is achieved. That effort can be determined as necessary or not which will be the deciding factor for you being able to sell a high ticket item, package or service, in the tens of thousands of dollars for instance. Thus it is a very powerful form when combined with direct contact. If the person does not seem interested but is still on the line, go ahead and ask if they have anyone in their contacts who might be, something you should do soon after you get a commitment as well. The same goes with DMs and even if you do close the sale, you still want to get any referrals you can, even potentially offering a finder's fee or equivalent to sweeten the deal.

In certain cases you may come across highly experienced sales, marketing and businesspeople who may not want to buy right now, but perhaps later, and if even not then provide you not only with some contacts but excellent tips, strategies and things to look out for to do even better when prospecting the next potential client; which in fact is more valuable than the potential revenue generated on any single sale. Therefore where you cannot convert on one thing, you can still learn or even develop potential partnerships. Remember a sale is not always money based, sometimes it is reflected in convincing another to take a specific action that can improve your brand or business in the future with incentive for that person or company. Whether you are focused on monetary transactions or even bartering, the point is genuinely mutual benefit; so your mission, strategy and style are all up to you.

Contests & Giveaways

Although contests and giveaways are often suggested as ways to increase engagement, the cold, hard reality is that running a contest or giveaway takes just as much energy and effort as trying to sell something. Although you may not have to go as deep in terms of questioning and prodding people as you do in the next chapter specifically dealing with selling you still need to do all of the above up until this point for the contests and giveaways to really click. They still need to be run like full-on campaigns. Never expect that the moment you are offering a free prize, no matter how cool or in demand, that people will just start flocking, the truth is people are just too distracted, too lazy and too suspicious most of the time, moreover most people will not really catch on until they have already heard about it in advance a dozen times. You would think that offering something for free would be a no-brainer for getting more people excited and paying attention, but the reality is whenever there are any kinds of sweepstakes or prizes to be won, the automatic question in each person's mind tends to be "what is the catch?" meaning unless it is super enticing and they have been expecting it, it is more likely each would give up on it in lieu of something more habitual and within a pattern that is accustomed.

This explains why big organizations and companies or even smaller ones with a lot of experience, will even go as far as paying a lot of money for adverts about the completely free offer or raffle and treat it with the same energy as classic marketing early on in order to get substantial participation and attention. So the question might be, "Why do it at all?" Though there is a huge amount of sacrifice and it seems that most are ungrateful for these opportunities without literally being bombarded by the hype, unfortunately it is often hard for people to break those mental patterns and usual expectations on top of having the trust plus your offer being a good particular match with the timing. That is why, whether you are going organic, paid or both you will need to use what Charlie Munger has coined as the term *lollapalooza effect* in order to really capture them into anything, whether it be your newsletter a free subscription to a private blog or even entry to win a free prize, no strings attached.

So what is this lollapalooza effect? Well it really is a combination of all the things already taught up to this point (on top of what is to follow, to at least some degree) coming at your audience from every possible conceivable angle, except this time not just to build your brand or increase general engagement to qualify for further prospecting, but instead to campaign a particular event that you want a good number of people to get in on. This can be used just as well for crowd funding or for selling, at least from a broad perspective (when excluding the following parts on prospecting which when combined is even stronger). The key is to understand this point that even a free offer without anything asked in return, say as a contest or giveaway to a random participant, needs to be framed and wrapped up in a whole media package, utilizing the social form on Twitter with polls, streams, memes, articles and more consistently put out there frequently for a substantial amount of time. Ideally with a lot of creativity and out-of-the-box experiments to really get the attention that this is a thing and that you are going all out to ensure everyone knows about it, 10+ times each from different angles at least. What may be effective and organized in achieving that is to have one central piece of content, namely a well edited video for instance, and to share that one Tweet featuring the video as much as possible, in as many ways as possible for as long as possible, inspiring related content and hype. No matter your approach, there should be an element of engaging content focused around one topic covered at scale, via all available means on the platform you can, whether orthodoxly or not.

To get to the answer of why you would not just use this strategy for something where you can make money and get some return on all that investment is that it is the ultimate way to brand yourself as highly generous, established and successful. All other reasons to implement such a strategy though potentially profitable still have an element of potential desperation, even if you do it in a way that makes it seem completely lacking such a need and that you are in a real position of power it still gives people a different feeling, knowing that you are "just like all the others" ultimately trying to hawk a product or sell them something even if you are the most awesome at it and some do convert and buy. This is all to say that doing such a thing, even knowing what it requires in terms of investment at a potential complete loss is an amazing thing to do for your audience if you can pull it off, so much so they will never forget it and it will be easy then to turn around, ask for testimonials and generate positive publicity about your brand. Even if they do not, doing good things without expectations can just feel exhilaration for your own self. It can be likened to a parent for their children, even though it is expected that you clean their poop on the daily, tidy up after them, teach them, cook for them, and still have to deal with complaints, disapproval and rebellion nonetheless, if you can successfully pull it all off, your kids will turn around, and be happy to do those things for themselves, and for their own children when they grow up never forgetting what you did for them especially when you have gone all out to communicate it kindly. With your business you can achieve the same with such an initiative if even at a micro level, to the point that your fans are no longer just potential clients or customers, they are your community, your culture and ultimately your evangelists, something that lives beyond you.

That is probably a way to look at it that may offer some real perspective, so just as a parent you have to give a lot in advance, and still it might not be appreciated, until you do not only do well at it for one time or a short phase but consistently throughout the entire process, it will bring people not only to buy in and even may get others to do so for you naturally. This makes you not just a passing fad, but unexpected. The key however is that sum-of-the-parts approach combined with unwavering consistency, that before you know it, you may not know exactly what one element it was that got them to come in, you just know that it works with you constantly putting it all together in a focused way.

Your Sales Presentation

Now that you have scheduled the call, live video chat or VR meeting, you have to make sure you are prepared to deliver a proper presentation. You want to make sure you define your end goal first before preparing your call. The objective is for the prospect to take action, become a valuable relationship. This presentation will not be static but dynamic, able to adapt to the specific needs of that person. This is done by having specific questions prepared to find out what exactly is the greatest challenge that he or she is going through. Be ready to work and implement on the spot. You can ask questions like this and make note at the beginning of the session (space left for response notes):

1. *What is the main reason you decided to come on this call?*

2. Is there anything you are uncertain about regarding my product or service?

3. What is the one thing that would keep you from investing in my product or service?

You will have prepared in advance all the different facets of your product or service, which you, as a professional should be well-versed in focused on your irresistible offer. When the prospect answers the first question, you will understand your greatest strength or the potential client's greatest issue that needs to be resolved. With the second question you will know which parts your call will need to focus on and address in order to clarify any points that might leave the person unsure. With the third question you can know your person's objections or complaints about what you offer so that you know exactly what to agree with as a common issue, but then provide the reasons why you are different and that is not any issue in any regard after all after you clarify. After covering all of the above in your call you want to end with a final question:

4. Is there anything else you are concerned with regarding your problem?

This fourth question will give you a reason to wrap up the call or presentation in a timely manner and offer the person the opportunity to ask you for the details of the commitment so that you can lead them through any further process. As you go through the details with them, make sure they are taking each step as you direct them, with the same tone and energy as your entire presentation up till that point. Finally after business matters are completed and confirm give the person a big "Thank you!" or "Best of luck!" and all required details for the following steps. Before ending your call ask the person if he or she knows anyone in their network who would also benefit or relate to your offers. Finally ask the person what he or she thought of the presentation and if there was anything you can improve before saluting the person goodbye and closing the call.

After you have done many such calls, you can begin preparing a *webinar* (or equivalent) script that takes the top reasons from question number one, the top points from question number two, and the top objections from question number three to write a long form presentation that covers all those facets from beginning to the end. In conclusion you can then frame it as a question that pauses and follows with a presentation of a stack. A stack is a list of benefits one by one based on testimonials and positive feedback you have received from your past clients, knowing what is of highest value to your market. This will then lead to a special offer for that group where you give them a discount or a bonus for being in this particular event. Ideally you can offer both an exclusive deal and added bonuses as well. This makes them feel they are receiving a special treatment for making the commitment to come now and live instead of later on their own time and is a reward for doing so. Now the call-to-action is made so you can open up a Q&A section based on the one-on-one call format. Except this time you are dealing with the main relevant questions from the group, from here you can review your entire presentation, shortening it to only the major answers you have just been given by all on the call. This ends with repeating the stack of benefits, the special offer and offered bonuses exclusively for those on, except this time you add a time limit to the offer, suggesting that the deal will be gone within a limited number of hours once the call is done, choosing the amount of time you think it would take the slowest person to go through the process if he or she started within the hour, which is usually 60-180 minutes. This condenses a lollapalooza effect immersing with value in one sitting. Though of course these same principles can be applied to different conventions and standards.

Be sure all receive their proper thank you's upon business finalization. Also make sure to offer a survey in exchange for future discounts or special offers to get feedback on how you can improve the presentation next time.

You may be wondering after that breakdown, how you can ensure "enough people show up?" That is a fair question. What you would do is connect the dots from all that was taught up to this point; with a large enough targeted following, your content strategy that determines what best engages in your niche and style, with the relationships and contacts you have developed and gone deeper with, in conduction with the help of collaboration, you can run a campaign with a rich media tweet that appealingly promotes the event ahead of time with a confirmation system by email or phone. On top of this follow-ups before the event are recommended for a better showing. The more follow-ups and written confirmations of the commitment you have leading up the to the event, the more likely more will show. This is especially true if you have several reminders soon before the event starts. If your event has a seat limit, it is better to oversell the seats a fair amount - but only with the best prospects - in order to get a decent turnout. If you consistently run campaigns and events your followers will come to expect them. As you keep your events and promos fresh and appealing, your turnouts will get better and better. It is also wise to remember that when you set a goal much higher than normal when inviting you are likelier to hit the actual results you wanted. I can testify that conversions increase by using live events and promos.

Selling Accounts

Now you can go meta and not only use your prospecting skills for selling to your audience, but to sell to other brands or influencers who have not grown their Twitter yet. This is especially possible since Twitter allows you to go as far as not only change everything about your profile's look from photos to message, but even the Twitter tag itself! That is right. That means after building a Twitter profile with one name, you can turn around and flip it to a client as another one suited to that client. You can also change the associated email as long as your current email connection is working before you make the change.

This only works though if the audience you targeted is in the niche of the client who would want to purchase it. This means you had to have followed the guidelines in this book well from start to finish - even better than I did before learning what I needed to teach you in it - to ensure you have a high value account from the start. This way you can avoid my mistakes and unnecessary hurdles that has made my progress more challenging, if more enlightening. The ratio of a larger following to the amount that I follow may be a selling point on the strength of my account, but that is way more advanced to ascertain. At least when in the niche of your client, it is a better bet, also with your being able to now teach the strategies contained in this book from your own practice, there is a lot of potential influence, marketing opportunities and business to be had by buying such an account.

There is also the benefit to the client that he or she neither has to learn how to grow an account nor the strategies you worked on to engage your audience, all he for she needs is to buy the account and maintain it, much faster! This is great for those clients that want an immediate genuine solution and have the money to back it up. For them I would suggest you practice a *narrow prospecting strategy,* prospecting them frequently over a long period of time as discussed since this is a larger commitment but is also higher value than any other related social media service.

Focus on the benefits to be had by buying an account, it is a lead generation machine, a marketing tool, a customer service platform, a news source, and a status increase. This is great for startups with a lot of capital, influencers new or inept at Twitter, anyone that needs marketing that is not yet "killing it" on Twitter yet has established a business or capital for their current ventures. This is like selling a car so without a solid referral you should expect at least 7-15 touch points of communication with the prospect before closing a deal, but it is worth it for the mutual benefit such a deal could bring.

The only caveat in selling an account is the potential loss of business you could potentially receive with the account. However this is not the case if you have no established product, service or business to market from your account. This is also not the case if it is one of multiple accounts you own and are not able to manage it due to your focus on another account. It is also not of benefit to you to keep if the account was grown under a niche you are no longer in the market to target.

If you bought a domain with an email specifically tied to this account, you can sweeten the deal by offering to sell the associated domain and email account together as a bonus, having their details transferred to the back end of the domain and email hosting company you are employing to do that. That would mean they also buy those services packaged with the Twitter account and continue to pay for them as needed afterwards at the regular monthly or yearly fee which is usually quite reasonable and far from the price at which you would sell the social media profile. This is true especially if you are careful to buy domains and hosting while unchecking the added frills.

After confirming sale you can even go as far as completely modifying the account to reflect the new owner so as to show the quality of your services. If you have other accounts which you are building, you can also make use of the client's referrals to sell even more accounts. This is a lucrative business but requires a lot of longterm thinking, consistent work and sales abilities.

Build-Engage-Connect

Consistency

When it comes to social media, a sure way to be ignored and fade into irrelevance is to be inconsistent with how often you post. Whether it be 1 time a day or 100 times, the more your audience can trust that you will have something new regularly, the more they are likely to look to you as a source of genuine content. This is a great way to differentiate yourself among other influencers and profiles. By ensuring that you are implementing the proper content strategy you can also give them a reason to engage with you consistently. You will be establishing yourself constantly as not just a social media profile or influencer but as a legitimate channel people can come to for a unique combination of content to satisfy their intentions or goals regarding your niche. This applies to all social media and Twitter is no different. In order to do this you are going to need the right mindset.

The way to look at this is to find that time of the day where you will always be able to post consistently to your audiences.

My suggestions for kind of content based on engagement? They are listed at the top of the following page.

1. Photography Or Memes

2. Live Streams Or Videos

3. Personal Shout-Outs

4. Articles Or Stories

5. Polls & Questions

That is in an approximate order of usual engagement, though most do engage most of the time when formatted properly. Photography, when highly appealing, relatable or funny can also appeal without the need of text one would use in a meme, captioning the picture superimposed over the image. However it is still a good idea to include a keyword or two in the tweet itself rather than only the picture in case you need to search out that tweet since it will be unsearchable without any words or tags associated to it if you ever want to repost when it has been lost among larger amounts of other tweets.

Memes are the first more engaging form of content. If it can be funny, insightful and visually striking with clear accompanying text, it has proven time and again as a mainstay of engaging content you can use as evergreen humour or on trending topics. Going out there and looking up engaging Twitter accounts you will see what kind of memes they post to get an idea and give it a shot. As you get better at figuring out what works based on engagement percentage, you can hit with some incredible results that can keep your memes in your content rotation for a long time. Cute animals with funny text, famous faces with unique statements or jokes, relatable humour with your own face or even very clear and relatable text statements over an appealing relevant background are all effective approaches for creating memes that will engage, even making it like a poster can work.

Live streaming is performed through periscope but can be seen by those without a periscope account (though they need the app to comment during the live session) and will automatically be tweeted and streaming through your Twitter profile once you go live. A great thing about these live streams is they do not end when the stream is over. They have proven time and again to be incredibly engaging and usable as content you can keep posting for a long time afterwards too. Covering trendy topics or those highly relevant to your niche, wrapping each piece in a story, even by the way you title it, will all also increase the chance of your audience paying attention and participating.

Polls usually do better with simpler, more general questions or those having to do with very mainstream subjects (your favourite genre of music?), those that are highly niche and specific (Who's your favourite black indie rock drummer?) will always get less engagement, but may still be worth posting for the data you received as the results of the polls, so there are different reasons to employ them. You have the option to change the amount of days and hours the poll will be up ranging from a minute to seven days and everything in between. However unless you are often retweeting the poll during its run, there are chances it will be missed by your audience, unless you have not posted anything since in which case Twitter is more likely to show it. By tagging related handles in your network in the tweet like a shout-out and including a contextual story, more are likely to see it and care. If you include an image, Twitter will give you the option to tag people without having to do so in the text part of the Tweet, giving you more creative freedom within the 280 character limit.

Story

In order to really establish your brand it is important that your audience knows, likes and trusts you. This cannot be done in one shot or in one night, it needs to be steadily built up day-by-day over a long period of time. Human beings resonate most with stories, no matter the personality type, and if you are doing so with humour, analogies, references and pictures, it is much easier for them to embrace that story. You always want to start with a hook, an open-ended intro that keeps them questioning, which you can do by setting up the backdrop. In terms of Twitter this could mean a poll relating to a project you want to start but are first checking in with what your audience will vote. Not only does this get you the insight you need to better know your audience through one of the most proven engaging formats, but it also primes your audience for what is to come. Also, you do not have to pack all choices into one poll, you can run multiple polls with the same question but different answers since Twitter is limited to 4 options per poll. In order to start and open your story through content strategy, let us get into how you should set up your polls.

Your question should be simple and easy to understand and not much longer than about 7 words. The choices should be clear and easy to comprehend as well. As mentioned Twitter's default "What's happening?" is truly the template for reliable engagement. You should choose the option to extend the poll length beyond the default one day, since, as discussed, it is an engaging format which you can retweet continuously while it still runs. This kills three birds with one stone, as you are providing content that engages, getting valuable data and promoting an upcoming project in the making all at once.

For example if you have a bakery and you want to launch a new baked good but are not sure what kind of baked good would appeal to your locally targeted audience you could ask "What kind of treat should I launch?" then giving four easy to understand choices (i.e. cupcake, cake, muffin, tart) ensuring that you are running the poll up to seven days and retweeting as often as what works with you. You can do several polls like this, launching one after the other to include other considered options. If four options is enough, of course that is not necessary, but if you have sixteen options then you should launch four polls at a time. This gets you a lot of attention, activity, interest and value for and from your audience. From there you need to look at the percentage of each choice when the poll is done. The reason to focus on the percentage over who won has to do when you are running multiple polls.

If you run one poll and the choices get 20%, 5%, 35%, and 40%, but run another poll where the choices got 50%, 42%, 5%, and 3% although you could just group all the winners as #1 with in each of their respective polls, in fact the one that got 40% is actually #3 between the two polls, since the second poll got 42% and that should be your #2 most popular choice instead of just grouping all the winners together. The reason this is important is because when you want to run a new poll after all the previous polls are done, you can group the top voted on poll results together in the right order without leaving the best ones out. If the top choice for your third poll is only 30% then that is actually below the second most popular result of 35% from your first poll and so should be placed under it, even though it is the winner of its own poll while the 35% result from the first poll was second place. So simply go by the percent value to decide the order rather whether or not the choice won. From there you can construct a final poll that pits the top four choices by percentage across all your polls to get the truth on which really is the most popular. Sometimes the top result will change so a *tournament of polls* like that is valuable.

The next part of your story is the punch-line and this could be done with some kind of conclusion. Once you know the top winner or winners of your choices, you can create a prototype baked treat product based on the top choice and take a quality photo of it. You can tweet out "Here is your lucky winner from the polling results!" and this has created a story that you have not only told but your audience has participated in. Since a picture tells a thousand words, and a quality picture of something your audience is there and ready to see in the sequence of being primed for it, it is an excellent way to multiply the engagement of having put up the exact same picture without the advanced polling or announcement.

Furthermore you could then run a campaign where you have it on discount exclusively for those in your Twitter audience, giving them the incentive to head on over to your shop or call to make an order. The more consistently you run these kind of stories the more your audiences will expect them, want to participate and be excited for the next revelation and chance to get in on an exclusive offer to buy more of your products. When they come in and tell of the Twitter discount, you know where they came from and ask if it is Ok to take a selfie with them or a photo of them enjoying the product so that can all be shared in posts to add to your story. Better yet you can record a video of them giving a quick review of the product on a smart phone and even provide them with another discount coupon if they go ahead and shoot that little testimonial themselves with their own device and send it to you.

Then you or a representative can, perform a live stream through periscope which will stream right into Twitter, recap the whole story about your ideas to launch a new project, the decision to polling and what choices to offer, the results and how you and your team felt, the process of coming up with the right treat based on the following's choices and then launching the product in store to create response. Then offering them the opportunity to get the special deal on the new product for a limited time as a gift for being a loyal audience. Finally you can add some humour by developing a meme, a photo of someone stuffing their faces with their new treat and within a fitting established meme template, saying something like "SO AMAZINGLY GOOD, YOU'LL STUFF YOUR FACE!" just for laughs while concluding that story with lightness and entertainment that is all part of that journey informs yet excites your niche to buy. You can even take this further by filling in the above gaps during the development of the product with some simple text tweets of your current progress developing it, just to ensure that your audience still has it in mind as it is being worked on, but do make sure that it gets executed in a timely manner to go along with the momentum of that story.

After doing this you can then develop a proper video ad that tells your story, who you are, what made you start a bakery where you have, why people love it and finally go into your community participation ending with those very testimonials and photos of happy customers that you got from doing the above. This ad will really resonate with your audience and encourage them to share it with new audiences in your niche to increase your expansion. You can also put that ad into a Twitter Promotional Campaign, with the option of it being done for you by yours truly, to have this moving story of authenticity, fun and community spread out to an even larger amount of potential customers within your target market (hey, at least I am trying right?). Finally you can take all of the above and turn it into a page not unlike an Apple product page, featuring the same content as your video ad for more engaging content, especially for those that love reading most in your network. This is also a great story for journalists and mass media, allowing you to not only publish this article on your site but have the potential to pitch it to other blogs, news websites and media organizations who are always looking for interesting stories from the community that touch the heart. Ideally you can even get an interview using all of the above experiences and story to deliver a brand that cannot be compared to any other.

That may sound like a lot of stuff to do right there, but if you keep the mentality of integration, hitting as many birds as you can with one stone, which you may see is a theme of my methods, it will be manageable to keep batting out enough content. More than listening to what influencers who are getting this right say, watch what they do and you will see how the state of flow can have you wrap up handfuls of content up in one fell swoop.

Attention To Detail

As you develop your content strategy and experiment, not only will you get a general sense of what is more likely to engage, you will also be better able to refine your strategy and gain the capability to tweak the tiny details that can make a big difference. For example my memes used to all have the same text in the Tweet as they did in the meme, but I started experimenting with related text in the tweet that was different to the memes and that multiplied my engagement. Though I still had high engaging memes before I started to do that, it now increased the consistency and multiple of high engagement. Another interesting thing is the use of GIFs as they can make or break the engagement on a Tweet, some text Tweets that have no GIF are actually more engaging while others may be ignored without an accompanying GIF, a feature now built-in to Twitter and quite popular among its user base, so you really have to test the waters to see what works for yourself. Also the time that you Tweet whether or not you tag someone in it, if it is an influencer account you are tagging, someone you have engaged with before or anyone else in your network where it might be relevant, it can be more effective than you think.

Otherwise small refinements, like lack of typos or spelling errors can make a huge difference. Thankfully you can just go ahead and delete your tweet and try again when you make an error. No need to worry about losing any engagement up to that point. Why? If it is truly engaging content, it should work even better when done right. However thinking outside the box is also important. Now that you can work with a full 280 characters, there is plenty of room for full-on poetry, more than ever before without having to link out to the full text on another page (an old practice that few still cling to today). When combining that poem with a meme it can be super effective, so try out creative approaches like that and see what kinds of results you can achieve. You are also able to post several images in one Tweet now so you can play with what combination of images and the order you apply them to your tweets to see what works best. That is because if you put 3 instead of 4 images, it will make one of those images (the first one) bigger than the other, so you can achieve different effects that way too.

You can even go as far as mimicking the style of offer or landing pages on websites using a Tweet thread. Though you have always been able to reply to your own Tweets to make a feed that way, nowadays Twitter allows you to add new Tweets with a '+' sign button under the tweet before posting, so that you can actually have a whole stream of tweets one after the other already ready to go out right when you send the first one. For example you could have the first Tweet you write with a catchy header and related tight video with an eye-catching intro, story and multiple perspectives to fit in that 2:20 min. limit but before even sending it out, hitting that "+" sign, putting a call to action with a link to actually receive something, watch the full video or learn more. Under that Tweet before sending any out, another added Tweet that refers to certification or background as to what makes you an authority in that regard. Further under that Tweet you can have a longer description, making full use of the 280 character limit giving more depth to the top video, actions and references by giving more context in text with that same Tweet featuring an attached image that is actually a meme that brilliantly reveals that same 280 characters' message but in a quick phrase and compelling image. Under that Tweet you can add yet another speaking of testimonials or others who have already gotten to know about the above, tagging them in that Tweet and including multiple images attached to the Tweets with faces of each testimonial and overlaid text on each picture quoting what they thought. You can then even before sending that all out have yet another added Tweet under that with a video of only the testimonials with a call to action and link in the text portion. With a final added Tweet you can have a general info about you and your company Tweet with links to that and related pictures or video to learn more. You should probably get the drift by now as it is even possible to keep going, but once you are done you click send and it all gets sent out at once in a neatly organized feed of Tweets that parallels the effect of a landing page.

As another example and a modification of the above, you could offer different menu items in each added Tweet, different options available in your service, a different story with each Tweet related around your one story, a series of memes on the same subject or even a series of episodes all accessible out of convenience through that one send-off. You can also tag different people in each piece in the feed, so the possibilities are as far as your imagination or refinements go!

As you can see, even with its focused minimalist design, now with all the little features available, using them together or each in a creative way allows for infinite possibilities, you just need to be able to see the forest for the trees to innovate on what to do, have your content strategy stand out, making your brand a distinct voice in the Twitter-verse. So get well-versed in Twitter and you too will be Twitter-versal! (Please accept my apology for that one.) This way you are not only an influencer in terms of followers, consistency and knowing how to sell, but as a completely distinct original that no one can quite match.

Advanced Targeting

In the theme of going deeper with what can be done with the built-in features of the platform you can even target single individuals out of pooling groups of non-followers by using Twitter's powerful search feature in an effective way. This is great for finding partners, clients or mentors in a way that is less about getting them to come to you but you finding them, a strategy that although may be extremely potent can have inconsistent results in engagement and should be done only during limited amounts of time after using all of the above strategies consistently already first. The reason is that this works like a gamble or volatile high risk investment so it is better to be done with surplus incomes rather than your core resources. However this may also get you massive deals that could not be found any other way.

NOTE: This may be hard to understand or properly implement without already practicing & attaining some level of competence in disciplines taught before this section.

Three Questions For Extremely Targeted Prospects

1. Are you in currently satisfied with equivalent product or service?

2. Are you looking for a change or update within the next couple of months?

3. When's a good time to talk more in depth?

How To Find, Meet and Present Targeted Cold Leads on Twitter

a. type in keyword in search

b. find one that is attractive to you, ensuring he or she is authentic

c. especially if he or she is followed more than he or she follows, but that is not always set in stone

d. after qualifying use prospecting strategy, reaching out regularly until you get response

e. qualify further from there when you get a follow and can DM them the 3 questions f. if all goes well on first meeting or call, keep scheduling new calls or meetings, give each at least 7 hours total, pay attention to personality profiles

g. ensuring that you are the one inviting paying every time (e.g. coffee) in the last step, close your negotiations

h. ask to get referrals for new potential quality prospects

When delivering service put the customer's feelings and satisfaction first, it will be a better experience for the both of you. It is a great practice for understanding how customers and clientele think as well, marketing and selling, keeping that customer-centric approach in perspective. The reason you always pay first is so that there is no buyer's remorse, in the case the client ends up taking your product or service for granted or change your offerings or marketing that no longer appeals to that customer. Since you give so much upfront it is safer for any feedback potentially given, but never let it get in the way of your strategy, values or focus for your business in any respect.

You will need to set aside a certain portion of funds or be able to afford using the resources for this purpose after current responsibilities for your business and expenses. Here is an example of how you could limit your use of this strategy after already maintaining what else was also taught herein:

Calls/Meetings

- *Max 2-3 times a week*
- *Max 2 hour calls or meetings before closing*

Closing

- *Only after closing on current client quota, this would be a bonus customer*
- *Offer specials, promos and deals to these clients due to the colder nature of this strategy*

A challenging but real strategy whereby if you can get to the meeting stage the quality of the prospect is already high and potentially good to be loyal over the long term.

Production Hacking

The *Production Hacking* mentality comes from 3 major components that provides the mental framework for design, efficiency and effectiveness. Those three components are as follows:

1. Goals

2. Resources

3. Action

It starts with a vision of the finalized achievement and that is how one can form a goal-oriented approach, having a destination on the map of your success. It then comes down to earth looking at your present day resources whether massive or tiny, and either way researching, trial and error with wisdom in being resourceful employing whatever you can afford. Finally it is action, this comes down to executing consistently, in cycles to completion.

That is the way you can achieve a positive, sustainable and growing business that has a consistent direction, clarity and scope that really sets it apart, distinguishing it from any other. This also applies to your learning in a goal-oriented approach that is resourceful and executive.

Further it can be applied not only to the company culture and business but each finite project within that larger mission.

To give you an example, for one of my brand's the ultimate vision was to empower businesses with systems to allow them to sell better with a future-friendly platform for massive growth in the eCommerce industry. With sales learning and experience, the strategy was to prospect influencers on social media until a certain number is reached, train them to engage to campaign for the site while opening their own stores. It has a lot of potential with that format. If you have an eCommerce site setup it is not so hard to create new lower level administrators that can setup their own shop which you can charge a percentage on per sale.

Besides the above being potentially applicable for yourself, you can also see it as an instance of how it could work for your own unique business or project as well. Either way, whether on your own or with a team, you should ensure to have the energy to actually pull it off day in and day out. To prepare yourself, a system of meditation (or concentration), exercise (or extracurricular activity), with the proper nutrition and wellness become vital.

Starting Small

If you notice a consistent theme was that it was more important to start small, no matter how big your vision than to try to bite off more than you can chew, though keeping your vision massive and your approach intelligent. That would be basing everything on your strengths and then growing gradually towards small wins at first that consistently build up with bigger wins towards the direction of your ultimate destination as your compass.

Because this does not just apply to running a business but also each facet of life as well, each side supports each other. This can be applied to learning in that you can target to become a master in a certain philosophy, technical knowledge or history of a subject to provide scientific or anecdotal references to pool or calibrate your current perspective and deepen your comprehension. That is a big vision, but the strategy could be library books if you do not currently have a strong book collection, some libraries even having books borrowable online with a library card. The efficiency and resourcefulness is the point more than the particular method of doing so, so you will work from there. The point is to be able to take action immediately without excuses so that you are in the habit of doing massive things that you continuously target while constantly working on one piece at a time.

When I first started growing my following into the 10s of thousands, though it was gradual and not very consistent at first, it was neither random nor unplanned. I did set a target even early on that I would hit 10,000, though at the time I was so busy with many things I had no idea of when, just that I would keep working on it until I could hit that. When I did hit that I thought, "well let's double it to 20k…" It was only after I decided to go all in that I almost tripled that in half the time it took me to get there, but the point was I had a set goal and worked on it over time to get there, you should probably do the same if you are serious about achieving any of the above taught lessons in this book. With a combination of specific goals and an ever-increasing amount of consistency you will not only learn to hit them but how to multiply your results.

The reality is if I knew all of the content in this book - let alone the many other books and materials on this subject - I do not know how far ahead I would be today. You truly have ample tools to the point that just applying a fraction of what is in here will take you into the top 1% on Twitter. However you also want to set goals on not only what you can achieve in it, but what goals you want to attain with those newly developed resources. You may have built a following, got them to engage and even made some sales, but what about recruiting? How about a higher number of sales that you want to get? How about the promotion of a whole network of influencers you can collaborate with? How many influencers will you get on board? How are you going to get them to do that? As you can see your goals can go far beyond the basics of building the foundations of a business with Twitter, there really is the potential to scale up if you have the right mentality.

You can also take the data you gain from practice and experience implementing these disciplines to be able to better predict how much you will need to do to get a certain result. For example, I have found that for every 5 pieces of content, 1 is definitely going to engage above average, at least the way I currently do things, sometimes it is more, but usually not less. When it comes to video or stream replays it tends to somehow find a way to work out to about one view per share as an embedded DM Tweet (by simply messaging the Tweet's link as is, taught earlier). Results will vary and you will find your numbers, not only for engagements but finding partners or converting sales, the more you do, the more you can gauge what you need to do to achieve what you want, so make sure you have the goals in place, but that you also renew those goals based on what you learn in that process. Not only can you go for bigger and bigger plans, you can also become gradually more accurate when formulating them. Proactivity and reflection really pay off here and it is setting those specific targets that can give you the incentive to get there and know what it is really like in practice. Moreover if you set your target beyond your original goal, you are more likely to hit it, or even do better than that.

Absolute Focus

You are going to need to be aware of the nuances of Twitter when compared to other channels and keep on top of what are the current engaging styles by checking other influencers in your niche and what is doing well with them, at least from what you can tell, keeping in mind you are not able to see the accurate analytics necessarily, (though you can always enter in their Twitter handle on TweetReach.com where you do not have to register, log in or upgrade, just use the free report with their Twitter handle). They are supplementary to get an idea of what is working, if a less detailed assessment than having access to that very useful 1st-party analytics icon you can only check for your own Tweets. If you are friendly with certain profiles, you may be able to trade your analytics data that way.

Though this book has been focused on one channel, I wanted to mention that a lot of the aspects common to social media, marketing and sales can be applied elsewhere. As long as you focus mainly on one at a time you have a primary focus that allows you to get strong exponentially. This gives you a head start from transferring the higher level principles learned in getting good at one social media platform to the other. This is very much like learning and mastering programming languages where achieving a substantial amount of depth in one allows you to be able to more easily get better at the others. That is rather than trying to learn them all at once. If you do not reach any integral level of depth in any, it renders none of the others easy enough to learn and apply effectively.

The following and last chapter breaks off into some of the nuances on other social media and other channels to which you can effectively drive traffic from Twitter using all the techniques spoken about in this book. This works because when you focus strongly on one channel, you can expand from there instead of trying to hit all channels at once and having nowhere to anchor your network from.

Leveraging Channels

Blog

Out of all the different kinds of channels covered this is probably the most challenging one among some exceptions in that setting up your own blog does require some familiarity with platforms like Wordpress or other CMSs if not the ability to develop websites or web applications from scratch. However there is a wonderful service that connects right to your Twitter and leverages your followers called Medium.com which you can sign up to with your Twitter log in to get a powerful blogging system you can write, edit, post to elegantly share to any channel you choose.

The best blogs do a few things well. That is highly interesting or well-written content on engaging topics. Go from your greatest interest which has the greatest audience for an awesome starting point to hit that sweet spot between what the masses like and what you personally like. With powerful CMSs like Wordpress (or even Medium with its own learning curve) you can more robustly ensure to include images, with credits, video, audio, and downloads beyond the text articles. You can, and I would suggest to do so lightly, use advertisements with services like Google Adsense or equivalent to begin generating revenue before having a product on offer. It can also be used for eCommerce with the level of ease-of-use that SecureCheckout.Live (my own eShop) has and can also be great to learn for developing specialized technical skills. Medium has both the advantage of simplicity and ease of use along with its ability to have you reach a potentially huge mainstream audience via personally reported in-depth researched journalism within your niche.

Pick topics that you love, do research on trending content, news or pieces about that subject, looking through many and then polling your audience to see which idea they like best based on those references. From there the winner can be the choice for your blog post article. Otherwise fill a gap where you have faced a serious issue, but not seen it covered very well or neutrally online. You can then share that and have at the bottom of the blog, if prepared, a link to a landing page or any other campaign, movement, fundraiser, site or project you choose. You can even embed Tweets into your blog by opening the Tweet's options and choosing "embed" to get the code you can put in the scripting part of your blog post. You can also leverage a plug-in for automatically posting your Twitter feed live right into your blog, they are often updated.

If you post Tweets about content from your blog by using the strategies talked about in the section about paying attention to detail, and everything else, you can continuously drive traffic to your blog focusing on the Tweets that get the highest engagement using your developed content strategy. With that you can raise capital from pay-per-clicks with the ads on your blog, building lists to prospect, selling products or promoting services.

The following two channels are bread and butter communications to take your prospecting to that deeper level to leverage your status and strength in the Twitter-verse right to the personal channels like email, potentially enhanced with phone, to work with, learn from or provide solutions.

Email Marketing & Text

The reason I put blog posts as the first alternative was to lead into an integrated way to use your newsletter as a medium for interaction with your closest subscribers. When driving traffic to your blog you can feature a sign up form, that sends you their names and emails when filled out. The default settings on a system like Wordpress for example will also have it so anyone making comments has to give you their names emails and website. Either way, ideally you want it to be a focused list that understands it has signed up for your newsletter or email correspondence.

From there after finishing a blog post you can write a related or introductory email or text that links to the article, being careful not to include pictures or video in the emails as mailing filters can put this in the promo bin (oftentimes). You can also include a snippet of the article with a link saying "click here to read the rest of the article." This makes it quite integrated to have some newsletter content. That is without completely having to start a whole new story for the current day. Whether it be a link from a meme, mention of it in a stream or embedded video, you can drive traffic to your newsletter sign up form. Often the instant message prospecting also spoken about in this book is an effective type of strategy to encourage those close engagers to sign up.

You can of course also write emails or texts that are exclusive in content to the newsletter, perhaps even leading to an exclusive *member's only* page on your site just for subscribers. This is a great way to test new strategies before scaling them out, seeing if your products and pages are of interest and effect among your closest network. A great way to write an email is as if you are writing it to one of your subscribers one-on-one since it has depth and a personal touch followed by updating each email slightly to suit the needs of each reader.

This can also be done with a massive emailing app like Mail Chimp and so on, where you can set how each message is modified. This requires a lot of preparatory work especially if your list had already been built before going with the program, but after this initial hurdle it ends up being more time saving against sending out emails manually especially when your list starts to exceed 50-100 people where it starts getting more challenging to handle while taking care of everything else in your day.

Although embedded media content such as images or video is not recommended in emails, links to pages that have them is fine as well as standard text formatting, like using **bold**, *italics*, underline and so on but for texts emoji's may work as well, to have a more put together, dynamic or creative style. This helps your emails to stand out without being filtered out, showing that you go the extra mile to communicate your message while being relatable in your texts to be trusted in quality delivery of what you do. If you ever make the mistake of sending an email without a body, greeting the wrong person or meant for another account, you should always make sure to address it immediately once it has been found out with an apology followed by the correct email.

Though it is true that you do not always need to have contact by email or text to make negotiations and close deals, it often is the case that though people may find you or your offer on a mobile device, the likelihood of closing - based on statistics - is lower in comparison to when the person decides to "get serious," moving over to a larger device (tablet, notebook or PC) so email and offer pages can be more effective in those cases. Though over the last couple of years the rate of closing straight on mobile has been increasing, so the lollapalooza mentality is effective for covering all of that. Therefore it is not any one or more of these channels but a strong, nuanced combination of them all, driven by at least one main traffic source, your social media or offsite content. Expanding that out to multiple channels and variations, ideally to each prospect potentially convinces them to enter your world and buy into what value you bring that solves their problems, benefits them and improves their business and lives.

Just like any other form of content strategy, the same things apply such as the use of stories, humour, references, and more creative devices for deepening comprehensions and clarifying the subject matter in an easy to understand way. Therefore the chapter in this book on engagement applies here as well albeit with the limitations of not using rich media due to the email filtering systems as well as the fact that email has the closeness of a direct message with depth coming close to an article, thus giving it a different edge, allowing for a personal yet proactive approach. Thus you can apply the fundamental principles of social media marketing while being considerate of the specific context of each medium in order for the content to be effectively delivered natively and fruitfully.

Other Social Media

FB Groups & Marketplace

Facebook is very popular for its use of groups, an excellent way to build rapport through related communities to get yourself out there, create new connections, promote or even sell your content, through the Marketplace, which compiles buying and selling from the groups you are in or are local. It adds credibility and trustworthiness when you are seen as active in groups and part of your niche's culture.

Blog Posts

LinkedIn & Medium are great places to make blog posts from scratch, carefully paying attention to the proper formatting and editing process on each individual platform, you can also simply copy and paste the contents of your own blog's latest post and then link back to your page at the bottom of the article stating "originally published here." The bottom of the article whether on those platforms or on your own custom blog could lead to an offer page. Also, LinkedIn in general is a highly engaging platform as of this writing.

Stories

Instagram and Facebook are great places for sharing your personality through videos and images, but consistency and responsiveness are the key. You should be replying to the messages on your stories from your network every time. IG, though can be grown with similar strategies to Twitter, they are not as effective here where it is more heavily based on in-real-life connection making, advertising or stories combined with pure content strategy. You are best off making compelling comments on big profiles' content in your niche and focusing on stories as much as possible instead of growth hacking.

Streaming

Streaming currently is being pushed by many major social media and dedicated platforms so interactivity is high even with a smaller audience. Whether it is Twitch,

Instagram or Facebook live they all around make a perfect place to stream, a great supplement or simulcasting location when you are using Periscope to do it for Twitter while each can even be effective on their own. IG Stories and Snapchat, can also work in this way.

Variety

Bitchute is all about being dynamic so perhaps digesting content from your other social media channels in here may be an insightful experiment. You can also repost videos from Youtube, Vimeo or refer to Steemit posts. Otherwise custom content in multiple video lengths and formats can provide the grounds for taking advantage of burgeoning and content-thirsty platforms like that with growing audiences, so you have easier momentum in your content strategy, being early and strong in a new media broadcasting niche rather than facing massive competition on older sites like YouTube for instance.

Alternative

Gab is better for off-beat comments as a place for high engagement with less people but where the interface is almost the same as Twitter. Like Twitter it is easy to connect to new people. It just went through an entire overhaul and is now more functional and well-designed to keep up with Twitter than ever. Either way it is a mature platform that keeps steadily growing and is a worthwhile place for applying the concepts from this book. This is besides the use of other relevant platforms worth looking into like Quora for intelligence and Reddit for news or subcultural communities. Minds.com is a growing alternative social platform also worth looking more into.

Ads

You can pretty much apply ads everywhere as they are always potentially effective, especially if you emphasize the section on engagement here running your ad strategy like a content strategy, trying completely different styles of content and formats to see what hits best with audiences, doubling down on those into new models from there.

Impressions

A last point about engagement I wanted to save for the end was - not just considering the interest of your market but their personality will determine your impressions. If they are Twitter addicts, your organic impressions will be a lot higher than "sleepy but active" users who are on randomly on random days, if constantly engaging over the long term.

Why Twitter?

So now where does Twitter itself fit in all of this? Mainly four things besides the major influencers known to lurk there:

1. Articles

Racing ahead of Reddit as a source for journalism, it is a great place to share articles, news pieces and snippets to fans of similar interests.

2. Memes

Always proving engaging especially on this channel, it is a great place to have a lot of fun and try different things to see a different side of what Twitter brings to the table.

3. Polls

A very popular Tweet that should be made full use of for many reasons. It helps you understand your audience, accrue data, get interactivity, increase impressions and engagement. It is an all-in-one!

4. Ads

A much under-utilized feature of Twitter due to its challenging nature, being 2-4X as potentially challenging as doing it properly on Facebook which can take upwards of an hour to setup and can be pricey if you do not know how to ensure an ROI. By mastering engagement and conversions organically with the information from this book and applying what you learned there here, you are more likely to succeed when you pay to boost content.

5. Feedback

The Twitter-verse is a home for multiple; authors, writers, media people, copywriters, journalists, news outlets and owners within the realm of writing, so this book being discussed in a piece of content I put out there can be very appropriate. There are also as many niches on Twitter as there are industries in existence, from western medical healthcare to Japanese goth fashion, so whatever niche you are in - whether you are looking to drive traffic to your eShop or your own media website - can get instant feedback as to what people think in your niche. When you have grown an audience based on the strategies in this book, utilized the concepts for understanding your engagement while experimenting and getting creative to deliver what your market truly wants, you will produce the results that bring you to your ultimately desired vision. If you get a small amount of results, multiply those efforts to get that much more, and improve in the finer details to increase the impact of each effort.

Acknowledgements

This is a good moment to recognize those close to me that knew about this project early on who were positive and encouraging during its writing.

First to mind is my brother who expressed a genuine interest in this book on my first attempt at writing it while continuing to encourage me on my continuous attempts. Next would be my mother who was a large influence in getting me excited and immersed in reading and writing from a young age as an excellent communicator herself. My father deserves a mention for his technical advice. My uncle also deserves a shout-out for all his support that made such a project even possible. Finally my children, who are a massive inspiration.

You are all a part of this book.

9 781999 473518